Dolphins

Dolphins

Michael Bright

First published in 2001
BBC Worldwide Ltd,
Woodlands, 80 Wood Lane,
London W12 0TT

ISBN 0 563 53408 7

Produced for BBC Worldwide by
Toucan Books Ltd, London

For BBC Worldwide:
Commissioning editor:
Joanne Osborn
Editorial coordinator:
Patricia Burgess
Designer: Lisa Pettibone
Art Director: Pene Parker

For Toucan Books:
Commissioning editor:
Robert Sackville West
Editor: Liz Clasen
Designer: Bob Burroughs
Picture researcher: Marian Pullen

Cover photograph: © François
Gohier/Ardea

Printed and bound in France by
Imprimerie Pollina s.a.
Colour separation by Kestrel
Digital Colour, Chelmsford

PICTURE CREDITS:
Page 2 Innerspace Visions/Doug
Perrine. 6 BBC Natural History
Unit Picture Library/Barbara
Todd. 9 Minden Pictures/Flip
Nicklin. 10 Innerspace Visions/
Michael S. Nolan, TL; Auscape/
Doug Perrine, B. 11 Hedgehog
House/Paul Ensor. 12 Minden
Pictures/Flip Nicklin. 13 Still
Pictures/Roland Seitre. 14 Sandra
Doyle/Wildlife Art Agency.
15 Still Pictures/Roland Seitre.
16 Sandra Doyle/Wildlife Art
Agency. 16-17 NHPA/A.N.T.
18-19 Innerspace Visions/Armin
Maywald/Seapics.com.
20 Hedgehog House/Dennis
Buurman, TL; Innerspace
Visions/Robert Pitman, BR.
21 Hedgehog House/Barbara
Todd. 22 Sandra Doyle/Wildlife
Art Agency. 23 Still Pictures/
Roland Seitre. 24 Sandra Doyle/
Wildlife Art Agency.
25 Innerspace Visions/Doug
Perrine. 26 Innerspace Visions/
Doug Perrine. 27 Innerspace
Visions/Doug Perrine.
28 Innerspace Visions/Michael S.
Nolan. 29 Earthwatch Institute/
Kit Little. 30 Innerspace Visions/
Doug Perrine. 33 Innerspace
Visions/Hiroto Kawaguchi.

34-35 BBC Natural History Unit
Picture Library/Tom Walmsley.
36-37 Innerspace Visions/Doug
Perrine. 38 Innerspace Visions/
Doug Perrine. 39 Olive Pearson.
40 Innerspace Visions/Doug
Perrine. 41 Innerspace Visions/
Doug Perrine. 42 Innerspace
Visions/Doug Perrine.
43 Innerspace Visions/Phillip
Colla. 45 Innerspace Visions/
Doug Perrine. 46 Innerspace
Visions/Doug Perrine/
Seapics.com. 47 NHPA/A.N.T.
48-49 Innerspace Visions/Doug
Perrine. 50 Hedgehog House/
Ingrid Visser. 51 Auscape/Doug
Perrine. 52 International Dolphin
Watch. 53 Auscape/Becca
Saunders. 54 Minden Pictures/
Flip Nicklin. 57 Innerspace
Visions/Doug Perrine. 59 DRK
Photo/Norbert Wu. 60 DRK
Photo/Steve Wolper/Ocean
Images. 61 Innerspace Visions/
Phillip Colla/Seapics.com.
62 Innerspace Visions/Masa
Ushioda/Seapics.com. 63 Still
Pictures/Norbert Wu. 64 Minden
Pictures/Flip Nicklin. 65 Still
Pictures/Norbert Wu.
66-67 Ardea London Ltd/François
Gohier. 68-69 Minden Pictures/
Flip Nicklin. 70 Innerspace

Visions/Doug Perrine.
71 Innerspace Visions/Mike
Nolan. 72 Innerspace Visions/
Michael S.Nolan. 73 DRK Photo/
Doug Perrine. 74-75 Innerspace
Visions/Doug Perrine.
77 Earthtrust & Sea Life Park,
Hawaii/Dr. Ken Marten.
78 Earthtrust & Sea Life Park,
Hawaii/Dr. Ken Marten, T; B.
79 Earthtrust & Sea Life Park,
Hawaii/Dr. Ken Marten.
80 Dolphin Research Center.
81 Earthwatch Institute/Kit Little,
TL; Earthwatch Institute/Russell
Schleipman, R. 82 Earthwatch
Institute/Adam Levenson.
83 Tom Stack & Associates/Brian
Parker. 84 Wild Dolphin Project,
TR; B. 85 Minden Pictures/Flip
Nicklin. 86 Minden Pictures/Flip
Nicklin. 87 Minden Pictures/Flip
Nicklin. 88 Innerspace Visions/
Hiroya Minakuchi, BR.
88-89 Oxford Scientific Films/
Tui De Roy. 90-91 Still Pictures/
S. Dawson. 91 Sandra Doyle/
Wildlife Art Agency. 92 Oxford
Scientific Films/Howard Hall.
93 Hedgehog House/Dennis
Buurman.

Contents

1 NATURAL HISTORY   6

2 FAMILY LIFE   30

3 FOOD AND FEEDING   54

4 DOLPHINS AND PEOPLE   74

FURTHER INFORMATION   94

INDEX   94

NATURAL HISTORY

NATURAL HISTORY

As the diver entered the water, a dolphin suddenly appeared, postured, whistled and then made off. Minutes later it reappeared, repeated its dance and dived below. The diver followed, only to be confronted by a large shark that was heading straight for him with its mouth agape. His camera housing protected him from injury, but as the shark prepared for a second attack, two dolphins appeared, putting themselves between the diver and the attacker. When the dolphins headed to the surface to breathe, the diver was alone, and the shark began to tighten its circle. Suddenly, a third dolphin appeared, and then more, until six dolphins began to usher the shark away, their tail slaps accompanied by a cacophony of clicks and whistles. The diver swam for the surface. French wildlife film-maker Bertrand Loyer was that diver, and we know the story is true because the event was captured on film. Dolphins really do save people in distress.

Previous page: From October to May, leaping dusky dolphins can be seen from tour boats that ply the waters off Kaikoura on the northeast coast of New Zealand's South Island.

THE WORLD OF DOLPHINS

Dolphins have held a special appeal for humans since ancient times. Their perpetual smile, grace, playfulness and friendliness, coupled with their apparent intelligence, have endeared them to most people who meet them or have seen them in films or on television. Yet the reality of dolphins' private lives is only just being revealed, and the picture that is emerging from modern research studies is not always what dolphin-lovers have come to expect.

In biological terms, dolphins are small, toothed whales. They are related to the great baleen whales and are classified with them as cetaceans (aquatic mammals). But dolphins differ from baleen whales in having a protruding, beak-like snout and jaws with up to 100 sharp, conical teeth, one set lasting a lifetime. Dolphins also have a distinctive rounded forehead called a melon, and, with the exception of two species of right whale dolphins, a dorsal fin.

Most species of dolphin measure less than 4.5 m (15 ft) long, although the killer whale or orca, the false killer whale and two species of pilot whales

1. The bottlenose dolphin is the most common species to be seen in captivity. This individual is in a dolphinarium in Hawaii.

1. Hawaiian spinner dolphins leap clear of the water at Midway Atoll in the Pacific Ocean.

2. Atlantic spotted dolphins spend the day on sandbanks off the Bahamas.

3. A group of hourglass dolphins travels at high speed in the southern Indian Ocean.

3

are bigger. The male orca, the largest of the dolphins, can measure up to 7 m (23 ft) in length.

Like the orca, most dolphins are black, grey or brown above and pale below. Those inhabiting tropical and subtropical waters tend to have more complicated patterns than their temperate relatives. While cool-water species, such as bottlenose dolphins, are uniformly grey, warm-water striped dolphins have a flame-like striped pattern on their sides, long-snouted spinner dolphins have a distinct saddled pattern, and spotted dolphins, as their name suggests, are dappled.

Where dolphins can be found

There are about 32 known species of true dolphins in the family Delphinidae and five species of river dolphins in the family Platanistidae. Some, such as the orca, bottlenose dolphin and common dolphin, are found all over the world, but most species are confined to particular parts of the ocean. White-beaked dolphins inhabit the North Atlantic, for example, and hourglass dolphins live in the Southern Ocean. Northern right whale dolphins are found in temperate waters of the northern

Pacific, whereas southern right whale dolphins, unrestricted by large landmasses, inhabit south polar waters.

A number of similar species can be 'paired up', with one of the pair occupying temperate or polar waters in the northern hemisphere and the other in the southern half of the world. White-sided dolphins in the northern Atlantic and Pacific oceans, for example, are matched by the dusky dolphin in the south. Some of the smaller species have very restricted distribution. Peale's dolphin is exclusive to the southern tip of South America, for example, and the equally small Heaviside's, Hector's, black and Commerson's dolphins occur in isolated populations off southern Africa, New Zealand, western South America, and eastern South America and islands in the southern Indian Ocean respectively. Humpback, rough-toothed,

Fraser's, spinner and spotted dolphins frequent tropical, subtropical and warm temperate seas.

Of the larger species, melon-headed whales and pygmy killer whales are found, albeit rarely, in the tropical Pacific and Indian oceans. More common are false killer whales, Risso's dolphins and two species of pilot whales, all of which have a more global distribution.

The tucuxi is a former marine species, which was isolated from the sea by major earth movements in South America and is now confined to the continent's larger tropical rivers. True river dolphins are restricted to particular rivers or stretches of coastal waters. The boto shares the Amazon and Orinoco river systems of tropical South America with the tucuxi, while the franciscana is found in estuaries and inshore waters of Brazil, Uruguay and Argentina close to the

1

1. The Amazon river dolphin, or boto, is found throughout the Amazon and Orinoco river systems in South America, and may be found as far as 3000 km (1865 miles) from the sea.

2. Irrawaddy dolphins frequent estuaries and coastal waters in southern Asia. This pair is in the Mekong River, Cambodia.

2

La Plata river mouth. Although now extremely rare, river dolphins also appear in the major rivers of India, Pakistan and Bangladesh, and in the Yangtze river system and adjacent lakes in China.

Close cousins

Several groups of toothed whales resemble the true dolphins but are classified in separate families and considered to be whales or porpoises rather than dolphins. Smaller cousins are the porpoises. Rarely longer than 2 m (6 ft 6 in), they are chubbier than dolphins and have a blunt snout, small, low,

⭐ In ancient Greece, dolphins were held in high esteem and featured in frescoes and on pottery and coins. Their killing was punishable by death.

★ The Greek philosopher Aristotle (384–322 BC) recognized that whales and dolphins are 'provided with a blow-hole instead of gills', thus distinguishing them from fish.

triangular fins (except for the finless porpoise, which has no dorsal fin) and jaws lined with spade-shaped rather than pointed teeth.

A long, spiral single tooth, resembling a unicorn's horn, is clearly visible on the male narwhal, one of two species of Arctic white whales. The other is the beluga, known as the 'sea canary' on account of its constant chirping. Larger cousins include the bottlenose whales, which resemble giant dolphins complete with enormously bulbous melons, and the beaked whales, several species of which have never been seen alive: they are known only from specimens washed up on the shore. Beaked whales, along with the river dolphins, are among the most primitive living cetaceans.

PORPOISE BODY SHAPES

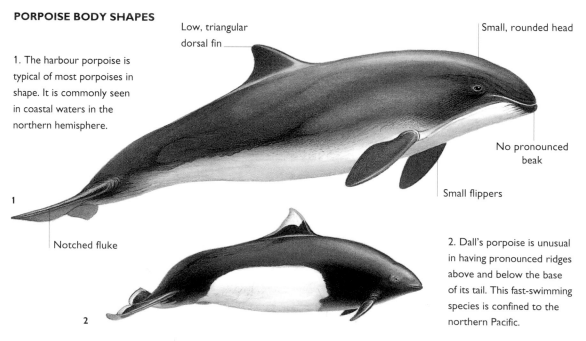

Low, triangular dorsal fin

Small, rounded head

1. The harbour porpoise is typical of most porpoises in shape. It is commonly seen in coastal waters in the northern hemisphere.

No pronounced beak

Small flippers

1

Notched fluke

2

2. Dall's porpoise is unusual in having pronounced ridges above and below the base of its tail. This fast-swimming species is confined to the northern Pacific.

3. The rare Yangtze River dolphin, or baiji, is found only in the Yangtze River and adjacent lakes in China. Fewer than 100 are thought to survive.

Prehistoric origins

Cetacean ancestors evolved from land-based hoofed animals about 50 million years ago. Most were herbivores, but a few were carnivorous and some omnivorous. They moved first into coastal swamps that fringed the ancient Tethys Sea, and then into the ocean itself, the earliest dolphin-like creatures taking over the ecological niches left vacant by marine reptiles, such as the ichthyosaurs, which became extinct 90 million years ago.

Modern dolphins are grouped into one of 11 families of living cetaceans. In geological terms, they are newcomers to the planet, having evolved as a group about 10–11 million years ago during the Miocene period. The traditional view is that the toothed whales – including dolphins, river dolphins, white whales, narwhals, the gigantic sperm whale and beaked whales – were closely related and were quite separate from the baleen whales. But recent DNA studies reveal that sperm and pygmy sperm whales are more closely related to the baleen whales than to dolphins. The studies also show that the ability to echo-locate (find their way by using sonar) was once common to all primitive whales and dolphins, but later lost by baleen whales. The beaked whales went their separate way early in cetacean evolution and are now only distantly related to the other groups of whales.

What all dolphins have in common is their streamlined shape and stabilizing dorsal fin. These have been tried and tested successfully several times during evolution, and the dolphins are the third major group of animals to have adopted it. First came the sharks, about 400 million years ago, followed 150 million years ago by the ichthyosaurs, and finally the dolphins, 10 million years ago.

PERFECT SWIMMERS

Everything about a dolphin's body is designed for the pursuit of prey. Shaped like a torpedo, powered by robust back muscles, and propelled with an up-and-down tail movement, a bottlenose dolphin swims with a top speed of about 30 km/h (19 mph), a spotted dolphin at 40 km/h (25 mph), and some individuals reach 50 km/h (31 mph) in short bursts. This ability to travel at high speed was once thought to be due to some magical property of dolphin skin. It is now considered to be the result of many combined factors, including body and fin shape, skin structure, muscle anatomy and physiology, and leaping behaviour. But the topic is still hotly debated by marine biologists.

Defying the laws of physics

At the centre of the controversy are some simple laws of physics. When a dolphin, or any other animal, travels through water, friction between its body and the water creates turbulence, which effectively holds it back. Turbulence is the enemy

2

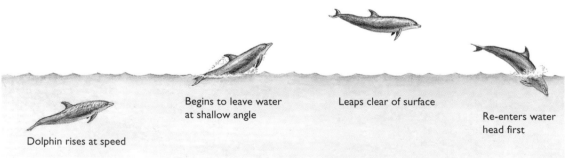

1

Dolphin rises at speed

Begins to leave water at shallow angle

Leaps clear of surface

Re-enters water head first

of speed. The faster an animal moves, the greater the turbulence that is created around it and the greater the resistance, or drag, that slows it down. It has been suggested that the dolphin overcomes this by tricking the water somehow that it is moving more slowly than it really is, thereby reducing drag and promoting a physical phenomenon known as laminar flow – the smooth flow of a fluid across a body without turbulence. This is something that all aircraft and submarine designers try to achieve. During their 10 million years or so of evolution, dolphins have gone some way to solving the problem, but how remains a mystery.

Proposed explanations include: 1) the skin cells are slowly but continually sloughed so that the dolphin literally swims out of its skin; 2) lubricating chemicals are secreted by the skin; 3) the water adjacent to the skin is heated up, thus changing its properties; and 4) the skin changes shape with changing speeds and conditions. But none of these ideas has been backed up by scientific research.

Studies in the USA and Russia have shown that a dolphin has small, regular ridges in the skin over most of its body, except on the snout, melon and lower jaw. They also revealed that the skin is well served by nerves that can detect pressure changes on the skin's surface. In addition, the muscles just below the skin 'vibrate' at amplitudes three to four times higher than those in human skin. These microvibrations, which occur at all times over the entire body of all warm-blooded animals, are thought to help maintain body temperature (shivering in humans is a natural extension of this phenomenon). But it could be that the ▷▷

1. In a behaviour known as 'porpoising', dolphins leave the water and travel briefly through the less dense medium of air, taking a breath as they leap.

2. Water seems to just flow across the body of this common dolphin as it breaks through the surface. By 'porpoising', the dolphin saves energy.

dolphin reduces drag by using amplified microvibrations in the skin to adjust to pressure changes on its surface.

Clues from glowing plankton

Scientists in the USA are trying to find answers to the mystery by watching how dolphins in the wild swim through swarms of 'red tide' plankton. These tiny plants and animals, which float or drift in the water, produce bioluminescence – they glow when disturbed. As the dolphin swims through the plankton, the greater the turbulence caused, the thicker the layer of bioluminescence around its body. Results to date show that areas of turbulence occur behind the blow-hole on top of the head, as well as behind the fins and tail flukes. Overall, the bioluminescence is brighter as the water flows along

Previous pages: With ears, mammary glands and genitals tucked away, the bottlenose dolphin is ultra-streamlined.

1. Common and dusky dolphins off the coast of New Zealand.

2. This bottlenose dolphin has an open blow-hole and is inhaling rapidly before closing up and diving below.

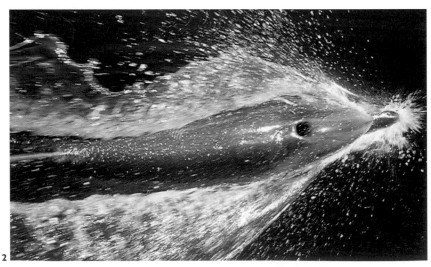

the rear of the body. The darkest region, indicating little or no turbulence, is around the melon in the dolphin's forehead. This is where its echolocation signals are focused and projected forwards (▷ p. 22). Most probably, this part of the body is shaped to hydrodynamic perfection so turbulence does not interfere with the transmission of its sonar signals.

Diving and surfacing

How dolphins dive has long puzzled scientists: do they actively swim when they dive, or simply sink? Dolphins can dive to 300 m (985 ft), stay down for five or six minutes, then return rapidly to the surface without getting the 'bends' (a dangerous medical condition caused by rising from the depths too rapidly). To achieve this, research shows that a dolphin starts its dive with a few powerful strokes of its tail fluke, then descends effortlessly. Its flexible ribcage and lungs collapse under the increasing water pressure, changing their volume and reducing their density so that the dolphin becomes less buoyant. Some oxygen is pushed into the windpipe and the extensive complex of nasal passages, but much is stored in the blood and muscles during the dive. Also, blood is diverted from the extremities when diving, and pumped to more vital organs. On returning to the surface, the lungs gradually expand, and as the animal reaches the surface, the nasal plug that closes the blow-hole is forced open, so the dolphin can breathe out and take in a fresh lungful of air. About 80 per cent of the air in the lungs is exchanged (compared to 17 per cent when a human breathes) before the dolphin dives below again.

 SURF-RIDING SAVES ENERGY

When dolphins accompany boats, it is more than just a friendly visit. They save energy by hitchhiking on the bow waves (below) and stern wakes of boats and ships. In experiments with dolphins trained to follow a research boat at the US Naval Oceans Systems Center in Hawaii, scientists were able to monitor their heart rates. They discovered that dolphins in the wake could swim twice as fast as when they swam alongside the boat, using little additional energy. It is thought they must have travelled on the bow waves of the great whales before people put to sea in ships. Dolphins also reduce drag and save energy by leaping from the water and travelling through the less dense medium of air each time they come up to breathe, a behaviour known as 'porpoising'.

'SEEING' WITH SOUND

Dolphins 'see' with sound. They bounce very high-frequency sounds off objects in their path and analyse the returning signals. In this way they can accurately locate an object, such as a shoal of fish or an obstacle in their path, determine if it is moving and in which direction, discriminate between objects of different densities – fat and bone, for example – and determine whether they are living or dead. They can even 'see' inside the human body and tell whether an individual is calm or frightened, friendly or hostile.

The sounds are heard mostly as clicks or bursts of clicks, which resemble a creaking door hinge to our ears. They are produced not with vocal cords but by pushing air back and forth through a complicated plumbing system of nasal sacs and plugs below the blow-hole at the back of the head. The sounds pass out through the fatty, bulbous melon in the forehead. This organ contains areas of unusual lipids, such as isoveric acid – a compound rarely found in other animals – which acts as a sound lens. The sounds are bent by the lipid molecules, focusing them into a narrow beam ahead of the dolphin, which can be directed where it likes. This makes the dolphin energy-efficient. The beam directs intense sounds on to interesting targets rather than spraying the area ahead with sound and listening out for something interesting to appear.

Interpreting the echoes

The returning echoes are picked up by an acoustic window in the lower jaw, where the bone is thin and transparent to sound. The signals pass through

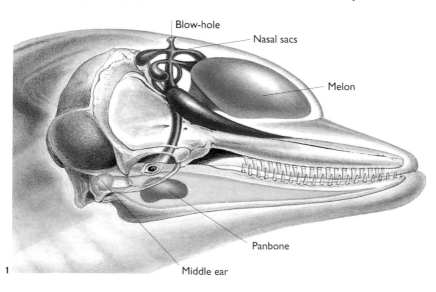

Blow-hole

Nasal sacs

Melon

Panbone

Middle ear

1

1. This cross-section of a dolphin's head reveals the intricate 'plumbing' used to make and receive echolocation sounds.

2. Good manners. All dolphins switch off their echolocating sounds momentarily if another dolphin passes in front.

2

a fat-filled cavity in the jaw, where the fat bundles are shaped like an ear-trumpet, and are transmitted to the middle ear, then to the inner ear and on to hearing centres in the brain via an auditory nerve that has twice as many nerve fibres as that leaving the human ear. It is thought that by using its jaws as a receiver, the dolphin picks up only the sounds it wants to hear, namely its returning echolocation clicks, and not the cacophony of other underwater sounds that might drown them out.

How, though, from the signals it receives, does the dolphin determine whether an echo is a meal or something less interesting? To find out, researchers in the USA have been testing how accurately dolphins can discriminate between objects suspended about 10 m (33 ft) in front of them. In one experiment, a blinkered bottlenose dolphin was able to differentiate between two small, hollow metal cylinders that were identical but for the thickness of their walls – a difference of just a few tenths of a millimetre. The dolphin did this by recognizing the time delay between the echolocation clicks returning from the leading edge of the cylinder and those that passed through and were reflected from the back edge – a time interval of just 0.5 millionths of a second.

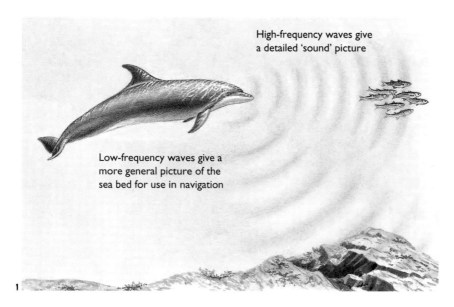

High-frequency waves give a detailed 'sound' picture

Low-frequency waves give a more general picture of the sea bed for use in navigation

1

1. The echolocating dolphin produces low-frequency clicks to survey its surroundings, and very high-frequency clicks for information about obstacles and prey.

2. Blindfolded with a suction cup, a dolphin retrieves an object using only its sonar.

Magnetic material in the form of magnetite has been found in association with nerve fibres in the head of the common Pacific dolphin, suggesting that dolphins might be able to navigate the oceans using the Earth's magnetic field.

Fine-tuning the signals

Theoretical physicists interested in chaos theory have also checked the data from these tests and, looking for order amid the chaos, have discovered that the dolphin tunes its clicks to obtain the best possible information.

It takes about six clicks to optimize the signal for the object it is interrogating. First the dolphin sends out a general click, then, depending on what it has found – fish, crab, boat, diver – it modifies the next click, the clicks 'settling' after half a dozen or so. The dolphin will not send out a fresh click until it has analysed the previous one, using the information it gained to modify its next click. Using this technique, the dolphin can detect an object, classify it and determine whether it is edible.

It is thought that the tailoring of these clicks should be more evident in the wild, so researchers working off the Florida coast have attached acoustic recorders to dolphins using suction cups and are recording their behaviour using video cameras. In this way, they hope to monitor a hunting dolphin's use of sonar as it detects fish, determines whether or not they are edible, pinpoints them precisely and catches them.

All these clicks are very high-frequency sounds, beyond the reach of human hearing. While the hearing range of dolphins is from 1 to 150 kHz (compared to the human range of 0.02 to 17 kHz), peak sensitivity is 40 to 100 kHz. Dolphins can hear sounds with frequencies below 1 kHz if they are loud enough, and there is speculation that tiny external ear openings just behind the eyes receive sounds below 20 kHz.

Touch, sight, smell and taste

Of the other senses, touch is surprisingly well developed. Dolphins frequently touch and caress each other with their pectoral flippers and their genital organs, not always with members of the opposite sex or even the same species.

A dolphin has excellent eyesight above and below the water surface because its lens and cornea can correct for the transition between water and air. The light-sensitive retina at the back of each eye contains both rods and cones, so a dolphin can see well in both bright and dim light, and can also see in colour. A tapetum lucidum, the mirror-like, light-reflecting layer that throws back light through the retina a second time, provides the animal with enhanced vision at low light levels. Two central light-sensitive areas, or foveae, on each retina – humans have only one – provide dolphins with binocular vision, the ability of both eyes to focus on an object at the same time. The position of the eyes gives almost 360-degree vision, with a narrow forward-facing field of binocular vision to the front but a blind spot directly behind.

2

Dolphins have little or no sense of smell, as olfactory nerves and lobes in the brain are missing. Taste buds at the base of the tongue and nerves going to the brain indicate that dolphins experience some sort of taste sensation. Experiments on bottlenose dolphins have shown that they can distinguish chemicals, such as different concentrations of citric acid, but they are poor at detecting salty and sugary tastes. Whether pheromones (chemical substances released into the water by animals) are important to indicate sexual or social status is unknown.

HOW INTELLIGENT ARE DOLPHINS?

The dolphin has a large brain, its brain to body-size ratio being comparable to that of humans. The cerebral cortex has a high degree of folding, comparable to that in primates, but while the neocortex layer – the part where most intelligence is centred – covers more of the surface of the brain than in humans, it is not as thick. This indicates that although dolphins may be intelligent,

1. Juvenile Atlantic spotted dolphins caress gently with their pectoral fins. Touch is an important means of social communication.

2. Male Atlantic spotted dolphins joust to establish which is top dolphin in a dominance hierarchy.

they probably do not 'think' in the way that humans do.

The level of dolphins' intelligence is a controversial subject in animal behaviour circles. Some scientists consider that dolphins should rank with the top three groups of intelligent animals – humankind and the rest of the higher apes being the other two. Some believe that all this brain power is the consequence of living in a complex world of sound in which the processing of acoustic information requires greater than normal brain space.

Echolocation and brain power

There is no doubt that one of the remarkable things about the dolphin's brain is its ability to process its extraordinarily rapid pulses of echolocation clicks. A series of clicks, known as a 'click train', might be delivered and received at a rate of 700 units of sound per second. The sounds would fuse together in our minds at 20–30 clicks per second, but the dolphin is capable of mentally separating these units, listening to individual echoes and decoding the information while interrogating its target. No wonder it has a substantial brain to process all this information.

What is more, the dolphin's underwater environment puts heavy demands on its brain. In addition to performing the normal cognitive (information-gathering) and motor (sending instructions to the muscles) functions, its brain must continually monitor how far away the surface is, how long the air supply will last, how far, how deep and how fast the dolphin can travel on one

2

breath, and so on. The brain must carry out a series of quite complex calculations even to make best use of a lungful of air.

Social intelligence

Dolphins are also social animals, and it takes brains to live in a group. You need to be smart to be able to compete, to deal with group politics, conflict and general interaction. Being a social animal is intellectually demanding, and there is some evidence to suggest that dolphins can use their sonar beam to scan their neighbours and evaluate their emotional state. Echoes from a beating heart, for example, will tell one dolphin whether the other

▷ PLAYFUL DOLPHINS

Dolphins in captivity have been seen to play with toys that they have made themselves. They blow air into water vortices to produce bubble rings the thickness of a drinking straw and about 60 cm (2 ft) in diameter. They push them about with their snouts and bite them, and even bounce the rings off the pool wall or extend them with a flick of their fins to create even bigger corkscrew shapes. In the wild, dolphins play with sponges. They grab pieces of sponge and place them on their snouts. They also play with sticks, seaweed (below), and buoys and boats at moorings, not only when they are young but even after they reach maturity. They share this unusual adult play behaviour with one other species – humankind.

is relaxed, tense or excited. Such a sophisticated sound system demands a brain that is able to process the sound information it receives, but the large brain does not necessarily indicate an advanced intelligence.

Yet having accounted for the brain space needed to perform these and other everyday tasks, there is still a part of the brain left over for being smart. A clue to this is contained in the brain volume to body-size ratio, known as the encephalization quotient, or EQ. Humans have the highest EQ, and not far behind are dolphins, chimpanzees and South American capuchin monkeys (the species involved in the Helping Hands Program in the USA in which monkeys do chores for handicapped people).

Self-awareness tests

Scientists have devised tests to establish intelligence in animals. Creatures are welcomed into the elite club of super-intelligent species if they can pass a simple self-awareness test during which an animal must recognize itself in a mirror. Humans, chimpanzees and orang-utans can do it, but monkeys cannot. The tests involve putting a dab of paint on the face. Chimpanzees quickly see that the paint is on themselves and touch it, but monkeys simply look behind the mirror for the 'other' monkey. The results with dolphins have been inconclusive: vision is not the dolphin's primary sense, so it is difficult to interpret results of the mark test in an animal that has no limbs with which to explore its body. Even so, in tests dolphins were seen to use the mirror to examine marks put on their bodies. They also brought objects to play in front of the mirror, and showed different behaviour in front of their own image than they did when confronted with a stranger. Researchers felt that these results were a good indication that dolphins are aware of 'self', but that more tests geared specifically to dolphins would be needed before they could be sure.

There is no doubt that dolphins are capable of performing complex tasks. They have good short-term memory. They are fine mimics and have even been taught to count in English and speak simple phrases, such as 'stop it', 'more', and 'bye-bye'. They can make out what a pointing finger means – a gesture that most other animals cannot understand – and they can indicate whether or not something is present. More importantly, they recognize symbols that stand for words and objects – both acoustic and hand signals are used in tests in captivity – and understand the order of words. They could distinguish 'dog bites man' from 'man bites dog', for example. This, according to some philosophers and linguists, is central to human language and a sign of intelligence.

1. Using both vision and echolocation, dolphins can recognize the shapes of many objects. Here an Earthwatch volunteer gathers together objects for use in tests with captive dolphins.

FAMILY LIFE

2 FAMILY LIFE

On the cliff-top above Kealakekua Bay, scientists watch and record the movements of a pod of Hawaiian spinner dolphins. The steep-walled cove was where the explorer Captain Cook met his end, but today it is a haven for dolphins. Having spent the morning swimming about calmly or resting in tight groups, the dolphins become active in mid-afternoon. Individuals dash about in a seemingly aimless way, and then, one by one, they start to leap clear of the water, spinning on their long axis for several turns before crashing back into the sea in a fountain of foam. This is a roll call. Each spinner is announcing it is ready to head for the open ocean and a night's feeding. With the register complete, the dolphins head out of their bay and join up with other groups to form hunting parties of 100 or more animals. In the morning the spinner dolphins return to Kealakekua Bay, where they are relatively safe from sharks and killer whales.

Previous page: Atlantic spotted dolphins may travel in large groups, but the main social sub-unit is a mother and her offspring.

ONE FOR ALL AND ALL FOR ONE

Dolphins are social animals. They live in groups, the size of which depends on species, age, sex and circumstance. Inshore species, such as the bottlenose and humpback dolphins, tend to gather in small groups of up to 10 individuals, whereas those living in the open ocean, such as common dolphins, congregate in their hundreds and even thousands, the result of many smaller groups coming together to travel or hunt.

Of the larger dolphins, false killer whales occur in groups of 50–100, melon-headed whales in groups of 100–1500 and pilot whales in groups of up to 50. Killer whales, normally found in pods of 4–40 individuals, can number 100 or more when several pods amalgamate temporarily. Whatever the size of the group, there are several advantages to group living: it helps in finding food, spotting predators and bringing individuals together for reproduction. It also spreads the responsibility and the energy cost of rearing offspring successfully.

Bottlenose dolphins' social etiquette

One of the most closely studied species is the bottlenose dolphin, the species seen generally in captivity. In the wild, its groups tend not to be permanent family units but unstable gatherings. Dolphins come and go regularly, so an individual might be with different groups at different times.

1. The members of this pod of bottlenose dolphins off Mikura, Japan, are probably not related, but individuals of the same age and sex may develop long-term bonds.

1

1. Atlantic spotted dolphins leap high and frequently as they take advantage of a boat's wake near Bimini in the Bahamas.

In fact, most of the dolphins in a group are unrelated, although more stable subgroups of 2–6 animals may stay together for longer periods. These can be mothers with their most recent offspring, who remain together for up to six years, or unrelated adults of the same sex or age who have formed long-term bonds, such as groups of sub-adult males, adult males or adult females without calves. Groups containing mothers and calves tend to be larger than those composed exclusively of adults or sub-adults.

Breeding groups usually contain only mothers and calves, but as a calf reaches maturity, it leaves to join a sub-adult group, where it refines its social etiquette, hunting techniques and sexual behaviour. Females may rejoin their maternal group after their first calf, but young males form separate bachelor groups. Two or three males from the same maternal group will often stick together throughout their lives. But fluidity between groups enables males to sample a larger population of females and so increases their opportunity to mate.

Hierarchy and dominance

Evidence from observations of captive bottlenose dolphins suggests that there is a hierarchy within groups. Males are dominant to females, and among females status is related to age. The older a female is, the higher she is in the hierarchy, and this might be demonstrated by the position she holds in the group. Dominant females and their calves occupy positions at the centre of their group, whereas less dominant individuals are pushed to the outside. ▷▷

Previous pages: A young spotted dolphin (recognized as young by its lack of spots) mates with an older female.

1. Rake marks from teeth on the skin of a male bottlenose dolphin are the result of recent altercations with other dolphins.

In the wild, the relationship between males can be variable: periods of low-level aggression are interspersed with periods of intense competition. During competitive bouts, dominance is established by jaw-opening, jaw-popping, bubble-blowing, teeth-raking and tail-slapping displays, as well as biting and ramming. Males have been known to fight so violently that one challenger will kill his rival. In order to avoid bloodshed, evidence suggests that the amount of white or unpigmented scar tissue on male dolphins is a measure of their 'quality' during aggressive interactions with other males. So the more scarring an individual has, the stronger he appears and the less likely he is to be challenged to an actual fight. A scarred male is also probably more attractive to females.

Social groupings worldwide

Few species have been studied as closely as bottlenose dolphins, but researchers are learning about the social arrangements of other dolphins. Striped dolphins in Japanese waters and humpback dolphins off South Africa's Algoa Bay region have a social grouping similar to that of bottlenose dolphins, but dusky dolphins off New Zealand and Argentina and white-beaked dolphins off Scotland occur in mixed groups of males, females and youngsters. Risso's dolphins and killer whales live in more stable groups. Risso's dolphin groups tend to contain one adult male and 4–6 females, with offspring of both sexes, and occupy the same geographical area, depending on the season.

How far will a dolphin travel?

Home ranges vary between species. Dusky dolphins off South America range over 1500 sq km (580 sq miles), whereas the home range of a well-studied population of bottlenose dolphins in Sarasota Bay, on the Florida coast, is about 85 sq km (33 sq miles), although individuals may range over much smaller areas. Bottlenose mothers and calves have the largest home ranges – about 40 sq km (15 sq miles) – while adult males, adult females without calves and sub-adult females range over 15–20 sq km (6–8 sq miles). Within the bay, subgroups have preferred areas, and membership of these groups can be relatively stable, the same individuals travelling and feeding together for up to four months at a time. The subgroup might forage among shallow seagrass beds for several days, for example, and then switch to hunting in deep-water channels for a similar period.

In other parts of the world, the same species might follow a rather different pattern. Bottlenose dolphins off the coast of southern Argentina, for example, might travel 300 km (185 miles) but will return to their original home-base, individuals feeding alone when inshore, but in groups in deeper water. Studies also show that there might be two subspecies of bottlenose dolphins with an inshore form, such as the Sarasota Bay dolphins, that hug the coast, and an offshore form travelling over waters that are 200–2000 m (656–6560 ft) deep. Satellite-tracking research has shown that the offshore dolphins travel great distances. An individual released in the Gulf of Mexico journeyed

2. Bottlenose dolphins have a very widespread distribution, but outside the tropics are most often found in coastal waters.

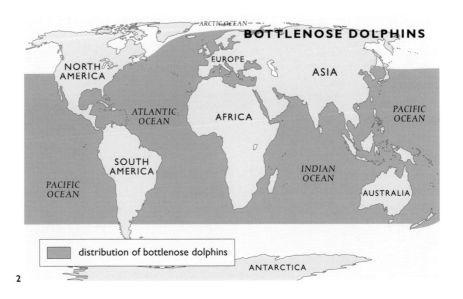

BOTTLENOSE DOLPHINS

ARCTIC OCEAN

NORTH AMERICA

EUROPE

ASIA

ATLANTIC OCEAN

AFRICA

PACIFIC OCEAN

PACIFIC OCEAN

SOUTH AMERICA

INDIAN OCEAN

AUSTRALIA

distribution of bottlenose dolphins

ANTARCTICA

2

around Florida and northwards to Cape Hatteras on the Atlantic coast, covering 2050 km (1275 miles) in 43 days. Another dolphin was tracked for 4200 km (2610 miles) in 47 days.

Mingling with other species

Some dolphin groups mix with other species. Bottlenose dolphins have been seen accompanying sperm whales, grey whales, right whales and humpback dolphins. These associations tend to be brief, lasting only for a few days, but some are more enduring. A single common dolphin has been seen with bottlenose dolphins for two years running, a spinner dolphin with bottlenose dolphins for four years, and a long-finned pilot whale with a group of Atlantic white-sided dolphins for six consecutive years. Why these individuals should take up with 'alien' groups is unknown.

DOLPHINS HAVE NAMES

When wild dolphins leave and rejoin groups, a simple procedure enables them to be accepted or re-accepted by the group: they use mimicry. All dolphins communicate using complex sound signals, and each dolphin has its own 'signature whistle', a collection of clicks and whistles which is in effect, its name. When it produces its own distinct set of whistles, another dolphin a few hundred metres away will copy it. After contact has been made, the dolphins continue the conversation with other whistles. When alone or separated from its group, an individual dolphin will call out its name for 60–90 per cent of the time, but as soon as others gather round, name-calling drops to 1–2 per cent of the time, indicating that signature whistles have some function beyond individual recognition in maintaining group harmony.

 SPOTTED DOLPHINS' CHARMED LIFE

The clear water of the Bahamas Banks is home to a closely studied group of about 50 spotted dolphins (right). They spend much of the day resting and socializing in smaller subgroups around the sandbanks, yet remain within 'shouting' distance. The water temperature and density 6 m (20 ft) down on the shallow banks provide an acoustic tunnel by which the dolphins can communicate over several kilometres. The mother-infant units are the tightest subgroups, a mother guiding her offspring with her body, a brush of her pectoral fin reuniting the pair if her calf should stray. Youngsters play, overseen by an older 'minder'. Any that fail to come when the minder calls with its signature whistle are vulnerable to shark attacks, and are disciplined with a tail slap.

1. The thin bubble stream coming from the blow-hole of an Atlantic spotted dolphin indicates that it is emitting its signature whistle.

Female dolphins create their own whistles, but a male dolphin adopts its mother's signature whistle. As males leave the maternal group permanently, this is unlikely to cause confusion, and if mother and son should encounter each other again, the same or similar signature whistle will prevent inbreeding, for the mother will instantly recognize that a male is related. The whistle is used when greeting another dolphin and to coordinate activities, often with great precision, and a dolphin will imitate another's whistle from some way away to attract its attention.

Some researchers have suggested that dolphin sound communication is so sophisticated that it might be considered a simple 'language', but despite all the recent studies, it is little understood. That dolphins communicate with each other at all was first tested in 1965, when a pair of bottlenose dolphins was placed in adjacent tanks so that they were isolated visually, yet could hear one another. The female was taught to push paddles in order to receive a reward. The male was given a similar set of paddles but had no training. Yet the male eventually pushed the correct paddle, and throughout the tests an exchange of whistles and clicks was heard. The experiment suggested that the female had been telling the male which paddle to press, but the researchers were never able to prove that the male had not worked it out for himself.

So many sound signals

What the experiment did reveal was the huge variety of sounds that dolphins make. There are squawks, whistles, squeaks, burps, groans, clicks, barks, rattles, chirps and moans. The bewildering array can be grouped roughly into two types: pulsed and unpulsed sounds. The pulsed sounds include ultra-high-frequency clicks and click trains that sound like rusty hinges, and broad-band burst pulses that have been described as 'Bronx cheers' or 'raspberries', depending on which side of the Atlantic you live. The more continuous sounds are the frequency-modulated whistles and squeaks. Dolphins can whistle and click simultaneously, and it was once believed that the pulsed sounds were echolocation signals and the continuous tones were for communication. Later research revealed that male bottlenose dolphins give pulsed 'yelps' during courtship, and frightened dolphins emit pulsed squeaks which may be alarm calls. Whistles and chirps are emitted during social interactions and play, while clicks and click trains are more evident when foraging or being generally inquisitive. Dolphins also whistle more when they arrive at a familiar place, while bow-riding or when they are under stress.

In research on captive animals, it was noticed that a spotted dolphin gave an almost continuous stream of whistles when captured, which scientists interpreted as alarm calls. The sounds were recorded and then played back to the group from which the individual had been removed. The dolphins fled immediately. The same calls were then played to another school, which showed mild curiosity but did not flee. The dolphin's own school had picked up a danger signal from the familiar call of the captured dolphin, whereas the strangers were unable to appreciate the significance of the call.

In another test in captivity, in which dolphins were again placed in separate tanks, it was discovered that while dolphins match whistles, their calls do not overlap. There was also a rhythm in the exchange: short calls passed quickly between two dolphins whereas longer calls were greeted from the other tank by long periods of silence.

2

1. (opposite) Open-mouthed threat displays and bubbles accompany 'squawk' vocalizations of a group of Atlantic spotted dolphins.

2. Bubbles from their blow-holes betray an intense conversation or even an argument between these Atlantic spotted dolphins.

Communicating feelings

Other research has revealed that dolphins deliver their usual calls in a particular way to convey their emotional state. Analysis of the calls from captive dolphins swimming normally and those from dolphins removed from the tank for veterinary examination has revealed that dolphins under stress emit calls that have a significant pitch or duration change. So dolphins, in common with several other non-human species, show what can only be described as emotional behaviour. Female dolphins in the wild and in captivity, for example, have been seen trying frantically to revive a dead calf. These studies also suggest that dolphins rely so much on their acoustic sense that they may be able to project their thoughts, in the form of acoustic rather than visual imagery, into the minds of other dolphins in their group.

GENTLE TOUCH

Communication between dolphins is not confined to sound signals. Touch and postures are important, too, and these can be used either on their own or to reinforce calls. Spotted dolphins in clear, tropical waters, and other species, such as bottlenose dolphins in clear-water tanks in captivity, use visual as well as sound signals, the postures and movements often eliciting touching and petting.

When socializing, spotted dolphins in the Bahamas posture and touch all the time. Compared to other dolphin species, they are relatively quiet, apart from long-distance calls between a mother and her wayward offspring, aggressive encounters, when sounds reinforce male head-to-head conflicts, and when orientating or foraging for prey. Young spotted dolphins also use what is known as

 DOLPHIN BULLIES

Sex and violence are rife in the dolphin's world. In Shark Bay, Western Australia, gangs of male bottlenose dolphins will kidnap a female from her group and keep her prisoner for a month. Courtship is minimal. The victim is bumped, bitten and herded at will while the gang tries to mate with her. If a larger rival gang appears, the males enlist the help of gangs with which they have 'secondary' alliances. These alliances can be long-lived: members of a raiding gang stick together for up to 12 years, and coalitions with other gangs may last three years. In Shark Bay, a more fluid alliance of 14 male dolphins enables individuals to join gangs temporarily, the size depending on the opposition's strength. They often form into pairs and trios, but a gang of seven has been known. These alliances and secondary alliances are unique to Shark Bay dolphins.

1. (opposite) These bad-tempered Atlantic spotted dolphins are in a head-to-head face-off, their posturing accompanied by open-mouthed threat displays and squawks.

'excitement vocalizations', a combination of signature whistles and burst pulses. An excited or distressed youngster will swim rapidly and erratically, causing its female minder to swim alongside and touch it with her pectoral flipper. Generally the young dolphin calms down immediately, but if it continues shouting, its mother will swim in and brush it gently with her flipper – a reassuring touch.

A mother and baby spotted dolphin will swim along touching pectoral flippers, and two adults might touch flippers when meeting – much like people exchanging a handshake or a hug. On occasions, two dolphins will swim together,

one resting its flipper on the other, indicating friendship, perhaps. Mothers will summon their offspring to come for a rub simply by rapidly rotating their flippers. But mothers and babies aside, most touching and rubbing are between dolphins of the same sex or age.

Touch is taken to an extreme by bottlenose dolphins. They seem to use sex as humans use a handshake. They mate frequently, sometimes just in greeting, and use sex not only for procreation but also for enjoyment, so females mate even when non-fertile. Sexual play might include 'rostrum rides', during which one dolphin will place its beak into the genital slit of its partner and push the

1. Touch is as important as sound in dolphin communication, but is reserved for intimate conversations, such as those between mating couples or mothers and offspring.

2. Individuals in this group of Atlantic spotted dolphins give an open-mouthed threat display.

2

dolphin forward while emitting sonar clicks that seem to stimulate the other dolphin. Melon-to-genital contact is also observed between mothers and offspring.

Making the right approach

The way dolphins approach one another also seems to contain an important message. Approaches directly from the front or side, accompanied by loud calls, are considered aggressive, whereas an approach from an oblique angle is seen as less threatening. Tail slaps from females in front of amorous males can mean they are not interested, and if made at the surface when the dolphin is

upside down can indicate extreme annoyance. Minders use tail slaps to herd together their juvenile charges. If youngsters fail to respond, the rate of tail slapping increases until finally the exasperated female rounds them up and delivers a tirade of calls and tail slapping.

Another posture is the 'head turn'. When dolphins are on the move in tight formation, they watch their neighbours to the side and behind, so an individual at the back of its group can make a head turn and steer its companions in a new direction. If one dolphin makes a head turn, however, the group will not respond to a head turn by another member of the group soon afterwards.

BIRTH TO DEATH

A group that might swoop in and turn a few heads is a group of males with procreation on their minds. When female dolphins are receptive, males join the maternal group and mate with them many times before moving on, so females have numerous partners during their lifetime. The sexes are difficult to tell apart in the wild. Genitals are concealed in genital slits in both sexes, but females can be recognized by the mammary slits on either side of their genital slit.

Female bottlenose dolphins may begin to ovulate as young as five years old, although several years may pass before an individual has the physiological and social maturity to turn ovulation into a successful pregnancy. Females normally breed at 9–10 years old and males at 10–13. But there are exceptions: one precocious bottlenose

1

☆ Pregnant spotted dolphins eat the same food, mostly squid, as the rest of their group, but mothers suckling calves have greater energy requirements, so they switch diets, preferring energy-rich flying fish to squid.

female in a population living off Sarasota, Florida, conceived when she was six years old.

Gestation is about 12 months, and when pregnant females come to term they adopt a variety of techniques during labour: some arch their body and flex their tail, while others stand on their head with the tail clear of the water while they arch their back. Deliveries can last from less than an hour to several hours. A baby is born tail first, bottlenose dolphins weighing 15–30 kg (33–66 lb) at birth and measuring 70–130 cm (27–51 in) long. As mothers average 180–272 kg (400–600 lb), the ratio of baby size to mother size is very similar to that in humans. Like a human baby, the newborn dolphin

1. A spotted dolphin mother suckles her calf, providing fat-rich milk from a teat on her belly. The milk passes through a tube that the calf forms with the palate of its upper jaw, its tongue and the mother's nipple.

has a disproportionately large head, and is crinkled and striped from the way it was folded in the womb. It also has tiny whiskers along its rostrum, which disappear during the first few weeks of life.

Early learning

Generally, a new calf swims unaided to the surface to take its first breath the moment it is born. It breathes more frequently than its mother at first, but quickly synchronizes with her breathing and swimming pattern. 'Aunts' may help a baby if its mother is in difficulty, and failed mothers have been known to try to 'abduct' newborn calves.

Successful mothers can act very aggressively towards them. The calf's mother will use her tail and snout to guide the calf into its swimming position alongside her back just below her dorsal fin. By the end of its first day, the calf will learn to position itself close to its mother, where it can hitch a ride on the pressure wave caused by her body moving through the water. It need do no more than beat its flukes occasionally to remain in position. Its dorsal fin tends to be floppy at first, but it firms up after a few weeks.

Suckling starts immediately after the placenta has been expelled. A feeding bout will last only 5–6 seconds on average, but there may be 10–20 sessions

1. A young two-toned male Atlantic spotted dolphin attempts to mate with an older, spotted female.

2. A baby bottlenose dolphin is about 1.1 m (3 ft 6in) long at birth and is in vocal contact with its mother from the moment it is born.

Baby spotted dolphins are spotless when born, but have a two-tone colour when juvenile – grey above and white below. They acquire speckled spots at first, then mottled spots when reaching sexual maturity at about 11 years old.

per hour for the first few months. The calf finds its mother's nipples on either side of her genital slit, and as it has no lips with which to take a teat as human babies do, milk is squirted into its mouth through a 'tube' formed by the calf's tongue and palate and the mother's nipple. The mother swims along with the nipple tilted towards the calf, and after several feeds the calf is directed to the opposite side.

The milk is very rich, so calves grow 60 cm (2 ft) in length and gain 75 kg (165 lb) during their first year. In order to keep pace with her offspring's demands, a mother must feed more frequently, increasing her normal catch of 4.5–9 kg (10–20 lb) of fish per day to as much as 14 kg (30 lb).

When the calf is three or four weeks old, it changes its swimming position from alongside to underneath its mother. It will also spend more time away socializing – rubbing, petting and chasing – with other members of the maternal group, but rarely with males or sub-adult males.

Bottlenose dolphin mothers give birth all year round, although they tend to drop their calves in spring. In Sarasota Bay bottlenose dolphins give birth mainly from May to July, when the water is warmest, usually over 30°C (85°F). Calves are born with little insulating blubber, but by the time the temperature in the bay drops to 12°C (55°F) in winter, they will have increased their layer of blubber by 30 per cent. During this period, they begin to learn social niceties, and the first skill they acquire is the ability to talk to the other dolphins in their group. At first, they make faint, quavering whistles accompanied by tiny bubbles leaking from their blow-hole – sounds that will eventually develop into their own signature whistle.

By the end of their first six months, young dolphins will have taken an interest in fish, their teeth having come through at about five weeks. In Sarasota Bay, they play cat-and-mouse games with small pinfish (gold-striped porgies less than 25 cm [10 in] long) – catching them, tossing them and allowing them to escape, only to be caught again and again. But fish do not form a significant part of a young dolphin's diet until it is one or two years old – although individual mothers accompanied by four-year-old calves have been seen lactating, and pilot whale mothers have been seen suckling 10-year-old 'babies'.

2

The threats to survival

Dangers abound during the first year of life, and one in five Sarasota dolphins does not reach its first birthday. Older mothers are more successful than younger ones at rearing offspring. Mothers less than 15 years old lose half of their calves, whereas older mothers successfully bring up four out of five. Sharks, such as tiger, bull and dusky sharks, account for some deaths off the Florida coast, but reports from a study of bottlenose dolphins living in Scotland's Moray Firth and from observations on the Virginia coast, eastern USA, suggest that dangers could be closer to home.

The research, some of which was video-taped, showed that the relatively large bottlenose dolphins attacked and sometimes killed the smaller harbour porpoises with which they share the Scottish loch. They rammed the porpoises and tossed them into the air, causing massive twisting injuries when muscles ripped away from bones, but they did not eat them. Once the porpoise was dead, the dolphins lost interest and went about their normal business.

This eccentric behaviour was something of a mystery until it was noticed that the relatively small porpoises resembled baby bottlenose dolphins. This prompted the suggestion that these attacks could have been either cases of mistaken identity or practice runs for a terrible undertaking – infanticide. Post-mortems of many bottlenose calves revealed that fatal internal injuries and external scarring were most likely the result of attacks by other dolphins, probably males but possibly females. Further evidence presented itself

 LONE DOLPHINS

All over the world, lone dolphins enter protected bays and harbours. As often as not they befriend humans, swimming and playing with them but not feeding from them. The reason for this association is unclear. Opo, a young bottlenose dolphin in New Zealand waters, lost her mother, and with no group to look after her, she latched on to children bathing, and one 13-year-old in particular. Lone dolphins are vulnerable to attack by sharks and may associate with people for self-preservation, accepting humans as convenient dolphin substitutes. Some loners might be old dolphins that cannot keep up with their groups, others could be outcasts from dolphin society. Many loners are male bottlenose dolphins, such as Donald off Britain's west coast, and Fungie (right) in Ireland's Dingle Bay, who may have lost their travelling companions or been defeated in fights. Spotted, dusky, tucuxi, Risso's and common dolphins have also been observed alone.

1. Bottlenose dolphin mothers are very protective of their calves. They keep them close, retrieving any that stray.

when researchers witnessed an adult dolphin attacking a dead calf. In Virginia, nine baby dolphins were found washed ashore with their skulls, ribs and vertebrae smashed as if someone had beaten them to death with a baseball bat.

If the attackers were females, the killings could have been their way of reducing the population and surviving hard times when food was scarce. But the more probable explanation involved males. The male dolphins were intent on killing the babies of bottlenose females sired by other males in order to bring the females quickly into oestrus. Females are receptive within days of losing a calf and ready to conceive the aggressive male's own offspring. It is a devastating mating strategy

seen in lions, tigers and other social mammals. Reproductive success is such a powerful driving force that it leads males of these species to kill the young of others to boost their chances of siring the next generation.

Those young dolphins that survive the rigours of infancy may spend five or six years with their mothers, swimming together until the birth of her next calf. Females continue to reproduce for much of their lives, with calves arriving every two years on average. Twins are very rare. Bottlenose dolphins reach old age in their early forties, and die aged 40–50. Females live longer than males. Female pilot whales, on the other hand, cease reproduction at about 30 but live for a further 20 years or more.

FOOD AND FEEDING

3 FOOD AND FEEDING

The air is filled with the raucous calls of gulls and other sea birds that dive repeatedly or thrust their heads below the sea's surface. In the water below, shadowy shapes betray a group of streamlined predators rushing this way and that. They are dusky dolphins and they are hunting together. Their target, a huge writhing ball of silvery anchovies, is tightly bunched together, each fish trying to hide at the centre of the shoal. Cruising round the outside and clicking loudly, some of the dolphins herd the fish more tightly, while others take turns to dart into the shoal and snatch a fish. Gradually, more dolphins arrive – other groups attracted by the commotion – and in a cloud of fish scales, they tear into the struggling horde, each animal taking its turn and eating its fill. Then, just as suddenly as they arrived, the dolphins disappear, leaving the birds to clean up the fragments of fish flesh that float to the sea's surface.

Previous page: Dolphins target a fish-ball of tuna near Cocos Island in the Pacific. The dolphins corral the fish, spray them with sound beams, then pick off the casualties one by one.

SEAFOOD PLATTER

All dolphins are carnivores. They locate prey using echolocation, then chase it, incapacitate it with high-energy bursts of sound, and grab it in their jaws. Their long rows of even, conical teeth are designed for catching fast-moving prey. Most species eat fish and squid, but certain pods of killer whales take sea mammals and sea birds, such as seals and penguins.

Most dolphins have relatively small, sharp teeth and powerful jaws, which enable them to catch quite small fish. Lantern fish and squid, which rise from the depths at night, form a substantial part of the diet of ocean-going dolphins in warm temperate and tropical waters, whereas the cooler-water species take cod, herring, whiting, mackerel, capelin and haddock, as well as octopus and squid.

Risso's dolphins and pilot whales have broader jaws, fewer teeth and muscles concentrated at the front of the head and jaws. They feed mainly on squid, but also take cod and herring: they follow the shoals. The seasonal migration of long-finned pilot whales off the Newfoundland coast corresponds to the inshore movements of short-finned squid.

Diets vary between species, and even within a species food can differ from place to place and from season to season. Populations of the same species of dolphin living in quite different habitats adapt to local conditions and behave accordingly. A study group of bottlenose dolphins living in narrow, dredged channels off the coast of Texas, for

1. A bottlenose dolphin has 23–25 pairs of sharp, sturdy teeth in each jaw. They tend to be even and conical in young animals, but worn in older ones.

example, spends only 21 per cent of its waking time feeding on the abundance of food concentrated in its habitat. But another population around Sanibel Island off southwestern Florida lives in open bays and channels, where food supplies are patchy, and spends 36 per cent of its time feeding.

Some species, such as large schools of common dolphins, maximize their chances of finding food by looking at the surface for concentrations of plankton and prey fish associated with topographical features of the sea floor deep below. In the western North Atlantic, common dolphins patrol the Lydonia submarine canyon off Georges Bank. At night they move in closely spaced echelon (steplike) formation to attack the squid that gather at the surface. In the southern California Bight, between Los Angeles and San Diego, common dolphins follow undersea escarpments and mountains some 2000 m (6560 ft) beneath by listening for acoustic

activity from the fish associated with them. Here they find concentrations of anchovies and squid in winter, and smelt during spring and summer.

Feeding patterns

Some prey species have greater energy and nutrient content than others, and dolphins select these at certain times of the year. Squid are consumed mainly in winter, but the more nutritious fish are taken during spring and summer breeding periods. But fish and squid are not exclusive foods. Striped dolphins off the coast of Japan consume vast quantities of shrimps. Distinctive black-and-white Commerson's dolphins enter estuaries along Argentina's Atlantic coast in two and threes, and are often seen swimming upside down, scanning the sea floor for food in shallow water. Here they round up fish and catch crabs.

 KILLING WITH SOUND

The dolphin's echolocation system is so effective that a bottlenose dolphin in captivity has distinguished between a tangerine and a small metal ball at a distance of 113 m (370 ft). In order to do so, the trained dolphin produced such powerful sounds that they were close to the finite limit of sound. Any louder and they would have turned to heat. Dolphins also use these high-energy sound beams to kill or debilitate prey from a distance. The sounds are not the very high frequency clicks normally used in echolocation, but low-frequency 'bangs'. Any fish that have been zapped, swim in circles or remain motionless. On the Bahamas Banks, spotted dolphins produce medium-frequency 'buzzes' while searching for fish buried on the seabed. Eels that are hit jump out and then stop moving, as if stunned.

1. Using echolocation to identify and locate its target, a bottlenose dolphin pursues a shoal of small bait fish. Its sonar signals disable the fish, which the dolphin then scoops up with ease.

On Chile's Pacific coast, another energetic species fishes along the outer edge of the kelp beds and in the fjords. White bands on their flanks, and the torpedo-shaped body, rounded snout and sickle-shaped dorsal fins, reveal them to be Peale's dolphins. They travel at speed in groups of eight or nine, hunting for the kingclip.

In the eastern tropical Pacific, spotted and spinner dolphins feed alongside yellowfin tuna. The spotted dolphins and tuna feed in the upper layers at dawn and dusk, but the tuna join the spinners to feed at night, intercepting lantern fish rising from the deep sea on their nocturnal vertical migration.

The spotted dolphins of the Bahamas Banks, like their ocean-dwelling relatives, are active mainly at dawn and dusk, but feeding times are flexible. During the day, dolphins forage for flatfish in the sand. Calves, recognized by their absence of spots at first, learn to forage as early as six months old, when mothers and older juveniles will chase up a flounder for infants to catch. Lactating mothers, with their high energy requirements, eat more food than pregnant females, females without calves and males. During the afternoon they join all the other subgroups as they move off the sandbanks and head for some serious feeding in deeper water.

FISH-BALL SOUP

Food is 'clumped' in the sea rather than evenly distributed, so dolphins are more likely to find food if they cooperate as a group. In this way, they can cover a wider area and rely on the collective experience of the group members to help find food. A group travels in a broad formation in order to scan the maximum area using echolocation. The size of a group depends on the availability of food in the area. Common, spinner and spotted dolphin schools, which feed on large patches of shoaling fish, contain many hundreds of individuals.

These tight hunting schools, distributed over an area of ocean up to a square kilometre, keep in touch with whistles or by visual contact, and use broad-band echolocation clicks to search for fish shoals. Some species, such as dusky and spinner dolphins, leap almost vertically out of the water and crash back in with noisy splashes – a behaviour known as 'breaching'. This could be the means by which the dolphins keep in touch during the chaos of the hunt; or the splashes could help to steer the prey. Whatever the reason, the dolphins herd the fish to the surface into tight balls, then pick them off one by one. The dolphins work together as a team, performing synchronous dives and surface rushes, followed by re-grouping and further attacks.

Killer whales behave in this way off Canada's British Columbia coast. Noisy resident pods herd

1. Spotted dolphins on the Bahamas Banks use echolocation to find small fish buried in the sand, then 'crater dive' with their snouts in the sand to catch them.

2. Spinner dolphins head out to sea in the late afternoon to join other schools in search of large shoals of fish, which they corral and consume at night.

2

salmon that are returning to the spawning rivers, trapping them against the shore, whereas the relatively silent transient killer whale pods, which wander the ocean in search of warm-blooded prey, herd seals and sea lions. Inshore bottlenose dolphins trap their prey against the shore, often a gently sloping beach. Indeed, herding behaviour can be seen among many species, including spotted, spinner, common and white-beaked dolphins, but the schools of dusky dolphins found off the coasts of New Zealand and Argentina are the supreme exponents.

⭐ The common dolphin has about 50 pairs of sharp teeth in each jaw, which are used to grip slippery fish and squid.

Cooperative hunting

Each morning during the southern summer, schools of dusky dolphins move away from the coast of southern Argentina and head for deeper water in search of shoals of anchovies. The 15 or so dolphins in each group swim abreast at about 6–7 km/h (4 mph), each animal about 10 m (33 ft) from the next, so the group sweeps a swath of sea some 150 m (500 ft) wide. Using echolocation, they scan ahead for prey, and when they leap momentarily from the water to breathe, they watch for distant sea bird activity at the surface – a sure sign that fish are present. When a shoal of anchovies is discovered, the dolphins herd them together and start feeding, using sprays of ultrasound to stun and disorientate their prey.

If the dolphin group is small, they are less likely to keep the fish-ball in place, and feeding will stop after about 5–10 minutes. But the commotion caused by the leaping dolphins and diving sea birds, such as terns, gulls, petrels and cormorants, that

1. A spinner dolphin in a Hawaiian bay launches into the air as it takes part in the afternoon 'roll call' before feeding in the open ocean.

2. (opposite) A bottlenose dolphin uses sonar and speed to isolate its target in a school of bigeye scad in the Caribbean Sea.

accompany them attracts the attention of other dusky dolphin groups. As many as 20 or 30 groups might congregate, with 300 or more dolphins joining forces, their combined herding behaviour enabling them to feed for 2–3 hours.

After feeding, the groups interact socially, with individuals touching flippers or swimming belly to belly. But by the evening the small groups return to their night-time 'resting' sites nearer the shore, where they can avoid their number one predator, the killer whale. Near the shore, orcas cannot attack from below and the relatively small 1.5-m (5-ft) dusky dolphins can escape through the shallows.

Elsewhere in the world, other species of dolphin and sea birds behave in a similar fashion. Off Scotland's west coast, for instance, sea birds watch for the activity of white-beaked dolphins, whose daily bouts of hunting and feeding are interspersed with periods of rest. The dolphins are active each morning, pinning shoals of mackerel and whiting against the sea surface and scooping them up from below, while sea birds such as northern gannets and herring gulls pick them off from above.

Feeding associations between dolphins and sea birds are common. The dolphins trap fish shoals against the sea's surface, and in the confusion, or as the fish leap clear of the water, they are grabbed by flocks of birds. One species of sea bird, the magnificent frigatebird, takes the fish right out of the dolphins' mouths. At Paraty Bay near Rio de Janeiro, Brazil, frigatebirds swoop and attack the heads of tucuxi dolphins as they surface, forcing them to give up the fish they have just caught.

 RIVER DOLPHINS OF SOUTH AMERICA

River dolphins (right) live in murky river waters with near-zero visibility. Their eyesight is so poor that at best they can tell night from day, and yet they can detect a copper wire only 1 mm (0.03 in) in diameter. They rely entirely on sound to find their way and to locate food, such as armoured catfish and piranhas, using a primitive, short-range, yet very sensitive echolocation system with a broader, cone-shaped beam than that of sea-going dolphins. Unlike other dolphins, the river dolphin is highly manoeuvrable and has a flexible neck so it can turn its head and follow prey. It can also change the shape of the prominent melon on its forehead in order to vary the pattern of its sonar signal. With these adaptations, the river dolphin can pursue single prey items and catch creatures living on the river bottom.

1. A solitary bottlenose dolphin chases a surface shoal of bigeye scad, a species that commonly falls prey to dolphins.

INGENIOUS FISHING TECHNIQUES

While many species of dolphin herd fish into tight balls in order to feed, some groups use ingenuity or tools to catch a meal. The female dolphins of Shark Bay, Western Australia, place sponges on the tips of their snouts. The sponges protect against spines or stings of animals disturbed on the seabed, such as stonefish and stingrays, cover the delicate snout when foraging among jagged rocks and corals, and also help plough through the sand.

Bottlenose dolphins off southwestern Florida often fish alone and use 'fish thwacking' to disorientate prey. With their tail flukes, they kick fish up to 9 m (30 ft) into the air, maiming or actually killing them. Bottlenose dolphins on the Carolina and Georgia coasts of eastern USA chase fish towards mud banks and create mini tidal waves that sweep the fish up on to the mud, leaving them high and dry. The dolphins then surge right out of the water – always on their right side – and beach themselves. Using their right pectoral flipper ▷▷

Previous pages: Hundreds of sea birds converge where a feeding school of common dolphins has forced a large shoal of fish close to the surface.

1. Bottlenose dolphins beach themselves on the mud in a South Carolina creek, and grab mullet they have driven on to the shore.

1

to anchor themselves, they grab as many fish as they can before sliding back into the water.

Off the Florida coast, bottlenose dolphins herd mullet into shallow water, then wait in a row. One dolphin surreptitiously swims out and around the fish shoal, stirring up the bottom mud as it goes, and returns, having created a semicircular curtain of mud that acts as a wall. The trapped fish will not swim through the wall or leap over it. Instead, they leap from the water towards the row of dolphins – which open their mouths and the fish jump in.

Recent acoustic research, however, has revealed that dolphins do not have everything their own way, for their prey can hear them coming. It was once thought that fish could hear only low-frequency sounds, but tests with the American shad, a relative of the herring, show that the fish can hear up to 180 kHz and could well pick up dolphins' echolocation clicks.

In the wild, this acoustic arms race has been monitored on Australia's Great Barrier Reef. Here dolphins are attracted by the chorus of sound-producing fish, such as terapons, but as they approach, they slow down their echolocation clicks, as if trying to hide their signals and not alert the fish. But the fish are forewarned, and the chorus grows suddenly quieter and stops, re-starting tentatively only if the dolphins pass by.

Fast food opportunities

Dolphins are undoubtedly opportunistic feeders. Bottlenose dolphins will steal from fishing nets and lines, and in the Galveston Ship Channel, on the

1. Atlantic spotted dolphins use sonar to search for flounders buried in the sand of the Bahamas Banks. They 'see' right through the sand and locate their prey.

2. Common dolphins in the Sea of Cortez have learned how to herd and trap fish using streams of bubbles, as humpback whales do. They then swim into the 'bubble net' and scoop up the prey.

Sea-going dolphins sometimes succumb to the poisonous algae that form 'red tides'. The dolphins do not eat the algae directly, but eat fish that have the algae in their guts. The poisons accumulate in their bodies and they eventually die.

Texas coast, they follow shrimp boats, taking advantage of the wealth of bottom-dwelling creatures stirred up by the trawl. Females with calves often follow the boats, but take care that the youngsters do not approach too closely. A mother will leave her calf with another female while she chases the trawl, coming back a little later to return the favour. This 'fast food' helps mothers to meet their extra energy requirements during lactation.

Elsewhere in the world, dolphins also watch out for 'trash fish' from large commercial trawlers and fish factory ships, as do killer whales and pilot whales. Pilot whales are potential prey for killer whales, yet these two species have been seen competing for the spill from trawls. Dolphins also compete with sharks.

SHARK ATTACK

Obvious shark-bite scars on the bodies of Hawaiian spinner dolphins and spinner dolphins in the eastern Pacific indicate that these animals are often attacked by sharks. In Sarasota, about 6 per cent of bottlenose dolphins show healed shark-bite scars, and elsewhere other dolphins show damaged fins, flippers and flukes. Whether the sharks see the dolphins as prey or as competitors is unclear.

In Australia's Moreton Bay on the Queensland coast, researchers have been watching bottlenose dolphins that follow trawlers for trash fish and fish that fall from the net as it is hauled aboard. The dolphins are not alone: alongside them swim blacktip and bronze whaler sharks ready to grab the same food. Often dolphins emerge from the mêlée behind the boats sporting fresh wounds. Evidence suggests that these are acquired in the feeding frenzy, during which the sharks inflict slash injuries on any competitors, whether dolphins or fellow sharks, and are not about predation.

In the Moreton Bay study, only male dolphins came close to the trawlers. Females and their offspring kept their distance from the sharks. On one occasion, two male dolphins actually chased

2

a small shark, but as soon as a 2.5-m (8-ft) specimen turned up, the roles were reversed.

Generally, dolphins have a healthy respect for sharks. In experiments in the USA with captive dolphins and sharks, it was found that dolphins could be trained to butt relatively harmless sandbar, lemon and nurse sharks – species that usually eat fish – but they refused to harass a similar-sized bull shark, a species known to attack dolphins. Indeed, several species of sharks, including bull, great white, dusky, mako, blue, tiger and oceanic white-tip sharks, have been found with the semidigested remains of dolphins in their stomachs. Whether the sharks scavenged or were intent on feeding and deliberately attacked the dolphins is unclear.

There is no doubt that sharks do attack and kill dolphins. On two occasions, a shortfin mako was observed doing just that. Although the dolphins were present in large numbers, they did not retaliate and attack the shark.

In Moreton Bay, bottlenose dolphins have been photographed sporting large, fresh bleeding wounds that clearly were not slash injuries but signs of predation from great white and tiger sharks. About 40 per cent of dolphins have them, and large specimens of these two species, caught by sports fishermen in the area, were found to have dolphin remains in their stomachs. When a tiger shark was opened up in Sydney's Taronga Zoo, it had two intact 3-m (10-ft) dolphins in its stomach.

In Shark Bay, Western Australia, the resident population of bottlenose dolphins is very wary of tiger sharks. About 74 per cent bear scars from tiger shark bites, most attacks coming from sharks over

1. This bottlenose dolphin has a wound made by a cookie cutter shark, which feeds by taking circular chunks out of larger marine creatures.

2. A bottlenose dolphin harasses a nurse shark, seeing it as a threat or a competitor for food.

2

3 m (10 ft) long. Young dolphins are most vulnerable. Some 35 per cent of calves do not make it to their first birthday, and of the survivors, only one in every two reaches weaning. Tiger sharks are so numerous at times that the dolphins must make trade-offs between feeding in the fish-rich shallows and risking attack. In winter, the sharks are absent, so dolphins can hunt in the seagrass beds in the shallows, but in spring, when the sharks return, they head for deeper water, even though the fishing is less productive.

In the Mediterranean, about 80 per cent of great white sharks caught accidentally in nets or stranded on beaches were found to contain the remains of bottlenose and common dolphins. A female great white captured off Malta, for example, contained the unmarked body of a dolphin, intact except for its severed tail stock that lay alongside, together with a blue shark and a turtle, in the shark's stomach. Had the great white shark disabled the dolphin by biting off its tail, or had the tail been protruding from a net before the rest of its body was swallowed whole?

In South African waters, where beaches are protected by shark nets, not only sharks but also dolphins are caught. Many of the dolphins have shark wounds, as do 10 per cent of those caught accidentally in nets used by fishermen along the Natal coast.

Sharks don't always win

Sharks can be victims, too. In the 1950s at Miami Seaquarium, a sandbar shark, which was showing an unhealthy interest in the birth of a dolphin, was attacked by three males and rammed in the gills until it died. In the wild, spotted dolphins on the Bahamas Banks have been seen to harass and batter tiger sharks and hammerheads, seemingly playing with them. Similarly, a group of humpback dolphins was reported to have chased away a 5-m (16-ft) great white shark off South Africa's coast.

Killer whales sometimes take sharks. A pair attacked a small great white off the Farallon Islands, west of San Francisco. On another occasion, the late Jacques Cousteau was presented with the 'gift' of a shark by a pair of wild killer whales.

Elsewhere in the world, sharks and dolphins have struck an uneasy truce. Pods of pilot whales in the Pacific Ocean off Hawaii, for example, have been seen travelling with oceanic whitetip sharks.

DOLPHINS AND PEOPLE

DOLPHINS AND PEOPLE

In 1963 two scientists peered over the edge of a tank at the Communication Research Institute on St Thomas in the US Virgin Islands. Elvar the dolphin, spotting at least one familiar face, swam over and presented his belly at the surface. The animal was inviting the scientists to tickle him. One scientist obliged and scratched him several times, but on each occasion the dolphin rested a little deeper in the water. At last, the dolphin was too deep to reach and the scientist gave up, removing his arm from the tank. Instantly, the dolphin swam to the surface, raised itself up until it stood on its tail and, towering over the two men, clearly enunciated the word 'more'. Had he understood the meaning of 'more' or had he simply mimicked a sound that triggered the desired response? Either way, it was a momentous occasion for astronomer Carl Sagan and pioneering dolphin researcher John Lilly.

Previous pages: Children come face to face with captive bottlenose dolphins at Sea World in Orlando, Florida.

LEARNING 'DOLPHINESE'

People like dolphins. In popularity surveys they often rank alongside dogs and cats at the top of the list, and in a BBC survey of schoolchildren in Britain, the dolphin actually took the top slot. Yet most of those voting would only ever have seen a dolphin in captivity at a dolphinarium or a marine circus. Here dolphins are coerced into displaying human-like traits and entertaining audiences with tricks, but have these involuntary ambassadors for their species helped us to understand them any better?

Research with captive dolphins has been extensive, and most dolphinaria now have scientific programmes running alongside the razzmatazz. The pioneering work with dolphin echolocation took place at Marineland, San Diego, in the 1960s, when a dolphin named Kathy was blindfolded with rubber suction cups and invited to negotiate obstacles in her tank. Kathy picked her way with ease through a maze of poles, never touching one, and was able to locate small objects on the other side of her tank. And when presented with two veterinary horse capsules, one filled with water and the other with fish, she picked the fish every time. Kathy showed that she could interrogate her underwater environment using sound.

Touch-screen computers and computer sound-recognition systems are now part of the captive dolphins' world. At the Earthtrust Human–Dolphin Communications Project at Sea Life Park in Hawaii, such equipment is used to establish a two-way communication channel. The idea is to break down dolphin sounds into individual phonemes, or pockets of sound, with which to build a 'consensus language' between humans and dolphins.

1. Dr Ken Marten with one of the baby dolphins that take part in computer-based experiments at the Earthtrust project at Sea Life Park in Hawaii.

At the Human–Dolphin Communications Project, 'Project Delphis', in Hawaii:

1. and 2. A bottlenose dolphin interacts with a touchscreen, and postures in front of a large one-way mirror.

3. Dolphins appear to accept a TV image as a representation of reality.

3

Gestures and sounds

Nowadays, the more intense, long-term projects take place at specialist research centres, such as the Kewalo Basin Marine Mammal Laboratory in Hawaii. Here researchers have been investigating the intellectual competences of bottlenose dolphins since the 1970s. In order to 'talk' to the dolphins, the team invented two language forms: one a language of gestures expressed with movements of the hands and arms, and the other a language of sounds generated by a computer and played into the dolphins' tank via an underwater loudspeaker. Both gestures and sounds have been used to represent objects, actions, the relationships of objects, and so on. Sequences of these gestures are like sentences, and when presented in a different order can have different meanings.

The research has shown that dolphins can understand the instructions given with gestures and sounds, appreciate meaning and word order, act upon new, unfamiliar instructions, appreciate sameness and differences between objects and label items with symbols, and refer to objects that are not present. What is more surprising is that they can do it all when receiving instructions from a television.

The gestures are usually given by researchers standing beside the tank (they are blindfolded to prevent them cueing the dolphins about how or when to react by movements of their eyes or head). But in some tests the researcher's image is delivered on a television monitor viewed by the dolphins through an underwater window. Most animals, including dogs, cats and even chimpanzees, are unimpressed by television and pay little attention to it, but the dolphins respond immediately, even with no prior training or exposure to television. Although the researcher's image is only a few centimetres high, the dolphins act on the instructions as if it were a full-sized person they were watching.

The results from all the Hawaiian tests are impressive. One dolphin, for example, was presented for the first time with the complicated 'sentence' of gestures, 'Frisbee-fetch-bottom-hoop' (meaning 'take the Frisbee to the hoop at the bottom of the tank'). It ignored a ball at the surface and a hoop at the top of the tank and took the Frisbee to the hoop at the bottom. In tests, dolphins get about 85 per cent correct, and even the errors are related to indirect objects or modifier words, such as 'top' and 'bottom'. They get the general drift of the word combination, even if they are not totally accurate in their interpretation.

 DOCTOR DOLPHIN

Autistic children and those with mental disabilities who swim with captive dolphins learn up to 10 times faster and with greater retention than handicapped children not exposed to them. This pioneering research at the Dolphin Research Center in Grassy Keys, Florida, was tested for flaws many times, but the dolphins always came up trumps. It was suggested, for example, that immersion in water was the stimulus, not the dolphins. To test this, teaching sessions were conducted in the water with and without dolphins, and the videotaped results were compared. The water-work with dolphins evoked a greater number and a higher level of responses from the children. In an expansion into a Special Needs Program, people of all ages with disabilities or terminal illnesses find moments of joy in the water with dolphins (right).

1

1. A captive dolphin catches
a Frisbee during language
experiments at the Kewalo
Basin research facility in
Hawaii.

2. An Earthwatch volunteer
at Kewalo Basin invites one
of the bottlenose dolphins
to be spontaneously
innovative.

2

Of all the sea-going dolphins, Heaviside's dolphin is the rarest, with fewer than 1000 living in the coastal waters of South Africa and Namibia.

Memory and mimicry

The research has also shown that dolphins have excellent short-term memory for instructions they hear and for the behaviour that they and the research team perform. They can remember 'lists' of five arbitrary sounds in a rapid sequence. Long-term memory is excellent, too, with an ability to recall the vocabulary and grammatical rules of the artificial language of gestures and sounds they have

1

1. Pioneering dolphin researcher Louis Herman gives hand signal instructions to a bottlenose dolphin at Kewalo Basin.

2. Language trainer and bottlenose dolphin at Kewalo Basin take part in a research project on the dolphin's ability to process information.

2

learned. They imitate sounds and behaviour well, and can relate their own body image to that of humans, so if a researcher lifts his or her leg into the air, the dolphin lifts its tail. When watching television a dolphin will mimic what it sees, and while watching a basketball player, it will search the tank for a ball and then thwack it into a net.

The Hawaiian dolphins are also creative. One sign they are given is 'create your own behaviour', when they are encouraged to behave in a way of their choice. Another is a 'tandem' sign asking them to team up with a buddy. When this is given with the 'create' sign, the pair create new behaviour together. How these skills match what dolphins do in the wild is the subject of future research.

CLOSE-UP ON WILD DOLPHINS

In the wild, dolphin scientists have adopted the direct observation studies of wild populations in the manner of British researcher Jane Goodall and the wild chimpanzees. Wild dolphin populations become accustomed to their human observers, and instead of fleeing or attacking, they ignore them.

In this way, the life histories and communication systems of Atlantic spotted dolphins have been studied by the Wild Dolphin Project, based on the Atlantic coast of Florida (▷ p.40). The unusual clarity of the water over the Bahamas Banks has enabled researchers to observe and record dolphin behaviour unobtrusively over long periods.

The study was set up in 1985. One current aim is to use sophisticated computer systems in the field to communicate with wild dolphins.

Other research programmes already use advances in technology to gather data. There are radio transmitters attached to dolphins by suction cups; satellite-tracking devices attached to dorsal fins; thermal imaging cameras that detect stress-related temperature changes in the dorsal fin; three-dimensional and linear hydrophone arrays to record and locate vocalizations; DNA sampling techniques that tell us who is related to whom. All these advances offer researchers a window into the life and mind of the dolphin.

One of the longest-running research projects has been Sarasota Dolphin Research Program, on

1

2

1. The Wild Dolphin Project director and her associate study data on board the research vessel *Stenella*.

2. A researcher with the Wild Dolphin Project photographs spotted dolphins' markings and injuries to allow monitoring.

3. A dolphin has recording instruments attached to its dorsal fin on board a Sarasota Dolphin Research Program vessel.

Florida's Gulf coast. The year 2000 was its 30th anniversary. A major aim of the study has been to follow identifiable bottlenose dolphins through time. Its scientists, using photographs that record markings on dorsal fins, can recognize more than 2500 individuals. With this simple technique, researchers have observed the day-to-day life of certain individuals up to 600 times in 20 years, and they are now monitoring the great-grand-calves of the animals they first studied in 1970. An early revelation was that about 100 of the dolphins in Sarasota Bay are residents, and that other dolphin communities in surrounding waters occasionally interact with them. This has been important in assessing the impact on dolphins of human activities and drawing up protection plans.

Airships and acoustic tags

One concern is the impact of boat traffic, especially on young dolphins during the key birthing period around the Fourth of July celebrations. The Sarasota dolphins share their waters with more than 34,000 registered boats. By using a tethered helium-filled airship with a remote-controlled video camera to record boat-dolphin interactions from aloft, the researchers found that boat traffic does influence behaviour. Dolphins of all ages group closer together, change their heading, swim faster and dive for longer when approached by boats, especially in shallow water.

In other studies, the airship technique has been combined with a pair of hydrophones towed behind the boat to record ambient acoustic behaviour when

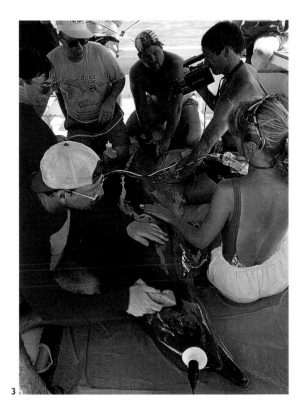

3

dolphins are foraging. In addition, on-board acoustic tags that record all the sounds a dolphin makes, including echolocation clicks, provide even more precise information about that individual's vocalizations and behaviour patterns. Acoustic data loggers are attached to the dorsal fins of dolphins brought in for veterinary examination, and they record speed, depth and temperature. An on-board digital compass also monitors the direction in which the dolphin is heading, and a battery of sensors measures pitch, roll and surfacing events.

1. A bottlenose dolphin with a hydrophone that enables researchers to record all the sounds it emits. The sounds are matched with video of its behaviour recorded at the same time.

2. Misha, a captive bottlenose dolphin, is returned to the wild after training on how to survive at sea.

From all the data recorded, the Sarasota research team found that single animals are noisier than those in a group, and that the sound signal of animals foraging alone varies according to habitat, different sounds being used in seagrass meadows than in channels. They also found that 58 per cent of the resident Sarasota male dolphins form tight pair bonds for life, while the rest remain single.

An unusual aspect of the Sarasota programme is the monitoring of a pair of captive dolphins that were reintroduced into the wild. The dolphins, captured in 1988 in Tampa Bay, Florida, had taken part in echolocation projects at Long Marine Laboratory, California. In 1990, they were released back into Tampa Bay after acclimatization at Mote Marine Laboratory. Both have thrived.

Elsewhere, similar research schemes are gathering information about other dolphin communities. South of Sarasota is Project Pod, a relatively new dolphin-watch project around Fort Myers Beach, Florida. After only a year, dolphin watchers discovered that their dolphins include a community of about 36 bottlenose dolphins that are not simply passing through but are locals.

In Australia, photo-identification studies, aerial surveys and general behavioural and ecological observations are being conducted at several coastal centres. At Moreton Bay, Queensland, for example, the local population of bottlenose and Indo-Pacific humpback dolphins follow shrimp trawlers for trash fish, and observations from the University of Queensland's trawler have recorded surprisingly aggressive behaviour between male dolphins competing for the fish. They push and shove, emit bubbles from their blow-hole, echolocate loudly at their rivals, nod their heads and clap their jaws.

On the southern Australian coast, the Dolphin Research Institute of Melbourne keeps tabs on dolphins in Westernport Bay and and Port Phillip Bay, Victoria. The study includes transects guided by GPS (Global Positioning System) technology, where boats cut across the bay in straight lines, recording dolphin numbers and behaviour as they go. One observation, however, has relevance worldwide. Dolphin researchers are concerned that the feeding of and swimming with wild dolphins has become an uncontrolled booming tourist industry.

HOW TO WATCH DOLPHINS

In US waters, it is prohibited to touch wild dolphins, and in other parts of the world researchers encourage people participating in swim programmes to respect wild dolphins, and not to chase or touch them. After all, it is not necessary to make physical contact with the animal: watching can be just as enjoyable and stimulating.

Anybody with access to the sea can watch dolphins and take part in fieldwork. Dolphins are so widely distributed that they are surprisingly easy to see in the wild. They are attracted to boats, riding the bow wave or wake, so ferries, cruise ships, pleasure craft and sailing boats often have dolphins alongside. They can be seen from headlands all over

2

the world, and they sometimes appear in huge numbers, such as the 1000-strong schools of common dolphins at Baja California, off the Scilly Isles in the UK or in the Straits of Gibraltar. The reporting of any sightings can be valuable to dolphin research, and many organizations coordinate activities of both amateur and professional naturalists and collect their sightings.

The Biscay Dolphin Research Programme, for example, set up in 1995, is run by a voluntary conservation body, which includes scientists and non-scientists who carry out year-round surveys of dolphins and whales in the Bay of Biscay and English Channel. One of the sponsors is P&O European Ferries, and observers use one of its regular cruise ferries, the *Pride of Bilbao*, as an observation platform. A display on Deck 11 informs passengers about the survey, and encourages them to look out for dolphins and

1

 FEED A WILD DOLPHIN

It all started nearly 40 years ago with Old Charley, a dolphin that herded herring under the old quay at Monkey Mia, Western Australia, making it easier for fishermen to catch them. The fishermen threw him titbits and he returned time and time again at precisely 07.15 every day. Other dolphins followed his example, and in 1964 a teenage girl on holiday with her family encouraged the dolphins, including an elderly female called Old Speckled Belly, to take fish directly from her hand. Today, dolphins still arrive at the beach (right) – Crooked Fin and her daughter Puck, Snubnose, Holey Fin and several others – and people from all over the world, including scientists studying the social behaviour of dolphins, can feed and touch these habituated wild dolphins.

1. Huge schools of common dolphins migrate regularly back and forth across the Sea of Cortez. They seek out areas of upwelling offshore where shoals of fish feed on nutrients brought up from the sea floor.

whales. The ferry follows a fixed route from southern England to northern Spain, and while crossing the Bay of Biscay encounters all kinds of cetaceans, including fin and sei whales, rare beaked whales and even pygmy killer whales. Common dolphin groups are seen regularly, often accompanied by bottlenose and striped dolphins.

Further north, the New Quay Dolphin Monitoring Group keeps a watch on a community of wild bottlenose dolphins that live in Cardigan Bay, West Wales. Dolphins here are often seen at dawn, dusk and just after high tide. Similar groups have been set up worldwide, and local wildlife societies normally have information on them.

Another way to watch dolphins is to become a research volunteer. There are several opportunities to join a research team and contribute to ongoing studies. An organization such as Earthwatch arranges for volunteers to join dolphin-watch programmes. At Sarasota, for example, more than 70 volunteers a year help to monitor the local dolphin community. They assist with photo-identification surveys, document births and deaths, watch for signs of injuries inflicted by sharks, and carry out surveys of fish that are dolphin prey. Similarly, the Wild Dolphin Project studying spotted dolphins off Florida's Atlantic coast, takes paying passengers on its winter cruises.

DOLPHINS IN CRISIS

Not all people love or respect dolphins. Some fishermen see them as competitors, others as a useful resource. In the Black Sea and in the Far East, dolphins have been killed in huge numbers for human food or cattle feed. In the Amazon basin the eyes of river dolphins are sold illegally as fetishes.

The fishing net menace

Drift nets, which form invisible curtains several kilometres long, catch dolphins indiscriminately. Throughout the world's oceans, 'ghost nets' (nets that have been discarded or accidentally cast adrift) continue to catch marine creatures, including dolphins, for years. Scientists in Britain have found a way to make these nets more 'visible'. A dolphin's sonar tends to bounce back from the swim-bladder of the fish it catches, so they are trying to mimic this by attaching small rugby ball-shaped reflectors,

⭐ The eyes of Amazon river dolphins or botus are valued as amulets by the Brazilian voodoo cult Macumba and are collected also as lucky charms by local people.

like underwater 'cat's-eye' reflectors, to fishing nets. Dolphins do not mistake the reflectors for fish swim-bladders and chase them. Instead, they pull up abruptly about 100 m (330 ft) away, bombard the obstacle with sonar signals, then swim around, over or under it. The clever device has yet to receive commercial backing.

Purse seine nets are particularly difficult to escape. They are legally used to surround and trap mixed schools of dolphins and yellowfin tuna in the eastern Pacific, and although the target species is tuna, the dolphins are inadvertently caught, too. In the 1980s, the USA began to crack down on tuna caught in this way, and many nations that trade with the USA were forced to modify their fishing

1

practices. Fine mesh net safety panels are now placed between the dolphins and tuna to separate them, and the dolphins can then escape through an edge of the net that is lowered. The result is so-called 'dolphin-safe' tuna. Although only 85 per cent of the dolphins escape in practice, the drop in dolphin deaths in the eastern Pacific has been significant – from 89,000 in 1990 to 33,000 in 1996.

Another fishing practice, that of trawlers working in pairs and pulling enormous trawl nets between them, is thought to account for more dolphin deaths. In 1994, a survey of mass deaths of common dolphins off the coast of southwest England, revealed that on one occasion 30 out of 38 carcasses washed ashore had abrasions and mesh-

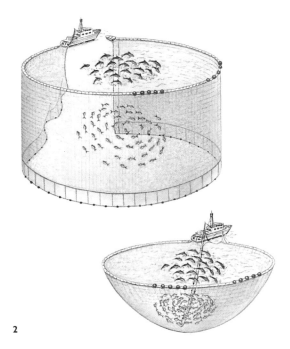

2

1. Discarded fishing nets, known as 'ghost nets', continue to catch fish and creatures such as this Hector's dolphin. Unable to reach the surface, the dolphin has drowned.

2. Huge purse seine nets are used to catch yellowfin tuna, but they also catch the dolphins that accompany these fish. A purse seine net is set as an open-ended cylinder (top). The cable running around the base of the cylinder is then drawn in (bottom), trapping the dolphins and fish.

like wounds around the snout and flippers. Several had flippers missing, suggesting they had been severed when being disentangled from the nets.

Widespread pollution

More deadly and more insidious than nets or harpoons is pollution. In parts of the world, such as coastal waters close to cities and chemical plants, dolphins and other toothed whales are seriously contaminated. Beluga whales in Canada's St Lawrence River estuary, for example, were found to have PCBs (polychlorinated biphenols) in their liver at a level of 500 parts per million, sufficient under Canadian law to classify them as toxic waste.

Dolphins in South Australia's Spencer Gulf, where the world's largest lead smelter is situated, have about six times as much cadmium (a by-product of lead smelting) in their kidneys as those living outside the Gulf. Off the coasts of Europe and North America during recent decades, epidemics of lethal morbillivirus (distemper) and mass deaths of dolphins, porpoises and seals have been attributed to poisonous chemicals, such as mercury, lead, PCBs from electrical installations and tributyl tin (TBT from anti-fouling paints) suppressing their immune systems. Tests on Dall's porpoises have revealed that high levels of PCBs and the insecticide DDT block the action of sex hormones, reduce fertility and lower the levels of lymphocytes, the cells that fight diseases such as morbillivirus. In the early 1990s, huge numbers of striped dolphins in the Mediterranean succumbed to the disease, as did bottlenose dolphins in the Gulf of Mexico in 1993.

1

The problem is that dolphins, like all large predators, are at top of their food chain. At each link in the chain (plankton–small fish–big fish–dolphin) contaminants become more concentrated, so dolphins tend to accumulate high levels in their bodies, particularly in fatty tissues. Organochlorines, such as PCBs, and pesticides, such as DDT and dieldrin, dissolve in fat and remain in a dolphin's fat reserves until they are needed for energy. During long journeys, or when food is scarce, dolphins call on their fat reserves, and a sick animal will use more fat than a healthy one, releasing even more toxins.

In 1999, a report on dolphin deaths in British waters showed a serious decline in dolphin numbers and above-average concentrations of toxic chemicals such as PCBs and mercury in carcasses washed ashore. Healthy animals that had been trapped in nets contained about 13.6 mg of PCBs per kilogram of blubber, while those that had died from infectious diseases had 31.1 mg per kilogram.

Young dolphins are at risk, too. The chemicals pass from a mother to her growing embryo during pregnancy, and then later she transfers even more to her offspring in her milk. A study of bottlenose dolphins off South Africa showed that in just seven weeks a dolphin mother passes on about 80 per cent of her organochlorines to her first-born baby.

Noise pollution

Another pollutant is noise. Humans add to the cacophony of loud underwater sounds. Among them are the low throbbing from the engines and propellers of supertankers and other commercial shipping, seismic explosions from geological surveys searching for oil and other minerals, and military low-frequency sonar systems that can track nuclear submarines across the ocean. In June 2000, mid-level frequency noises generated by the US Navy during operations in the Bahamas were said by cetacean experts to have accounted for bleeding in and around the ears of whales and dolphins that had stranded mysteriously.

Even perpetrators of benign science are guilty of noise pollution. In the Acoustic Thermometry of Ocean Climate project, sea temperatures will be monitored by recording the time very loud sounds take to cross the Pacific Ocean. Many of these activities generate low-frequency sounds that were once thought to disturb mainly the great whales and seals, but we now know that dolphins are also affected by loud low-frequency sounds. Whatever the pollutant or disturbance, it seems that dolphins are under threat and the problem is global.

Conservation organizations, such as the British-based Whale and Dolphin Conservation Society and the Humane Society in the USA, monitor dolphins both in the wild and in captivity, drawing the world's attention to their welfare, status and their natural history. It seems there are still people worldwide who care enough about dolphins to ensure their future is more secure.

1. At Iki Island, Japan, dolphins are rounded up and killed, then ground up for animal feed and fertilizers.

2. Dusky dolphins stranded on a beach on New Zealand's Kaikoura coast. The cause of dolphin deaths often remains a mystery.

2

FURTHER INFORMATION

BOOKS

Janet Mann et al, *Cetacean Societies: Field Studies of Dolphins and Whales* (Chicago: University of Chicago Press, 2000).
A review of the latest research projects about the natural history of dolphins and whales.

Mark Carwardine, *The Book of Dolphins* (London: Collins & Brown, 1999).
A general look at dolphins.

Peter G.H. Evans, *The Natural History of Whales and Dolphins* (London: Christopher Helm, 1987).
A review of cetacean research.

Wade Doak, *Encounters with Whales and Dolphins* (London: Hodder & Stoughton, 1988).
A compendium of stories about people diving and swimming with dolphins all over the world.

MAGAZINE
BBC Wildlife Magazine
A monthly look at wildlife and conservation worldwide.

WEBSITES
Whale and Dolphin Conservation Society
http://www.wdcs.org

Atlantic Dolphin Research Cooperative
http://members.aol.com.adrcnet

Sarasota Dolphin Research Program
http://www.moteor/~rwells

Biscay Dolphin Research Programme
http://www.biscay-dolphin.org.uk
Project Delphis
http://www.earthtrust.org/delphis

Project Pod
http://www.cetaceans.org

The Wild Dolphin Project
http://dolphin.wwwa.com

European Cetacean Society
http://web.inter.nl.net/users/J.W. Broekema/ecs

American Cetacean Society
http://www.acsonline.org

Australian Cetacean Organisations (links)
http://www.oceania.org.au/www links/auorg

INDEX

Italic type denotes illustrations

acoustic tags 85
Acoustic Thermometry of Ocean Climate project 93
Africa 12
    aggression 38, *38*, 44, 47, 52-3, 87
alarm calls 43
algae 70
Amazon River 12, *12*, 90
ancestral species 15
anchovies 56, 58, 62
Arctic 14
Argentina 12-13, 38, 39, 58, 62
Atlantic Ocean 11, 12, 58
auditory nerve 23
Australia 44, 65, 69, 71, 72-3, 86-7, 88, 92

babies *see* calves
bachelor groups 35
Bahamas Banks 40, 44, 58, 59, *60*, 70, 73, 83, 93
baiji (Yangtze River dolphin) 13, *15*
Baja California 88
baleen whales 9, 15
Bangladesh 13
beaked whales 14, 15, 89
beluga 14, 91
bioluminescence 20-1
birds 56, 57, 62, 64, *66-7*
birth 48-9, 51
Biscay Dolphin Research Programme 88-9
black dolphin 12
Black Sea 90
blood circulation, diving 21
blow-holes 14, *20*, 21
blubber 51, 92
boats
    influence on dolphin behaviour 85
    noise pollution 93
    riding bow waves 21, *21*, 87
    trawlers 70, 71, 86-7, 90-1
boto 12, *12*

bottlenose dolphin 9, 11, *18-19*, 89
    aggression 52-3
    blow-hole *20*
    breeding 46, 48
    calves 51, *51*, 53
    communication 41, 43, 44
    diseases 92
    echolocation 23
    feeding 57-8, *59*, 61, 63, 65-70, *65*, *68-9*
    gangs 44
    hierarchy 35-8
    home range 39-40
    life span 53
    lone dolphins 52
    mixing with other species 40
    pollution 92
    research 78-9, 79-80, *81*, 85, 86, *86*
    sense of taste 26
    shark attacks 71, 72-3, *72-3*
    social groups 33-5, *33*
    speed 16
    teeth 57
bottlenose whale 14
botu 90
brain 23, 26-9
Brazil 12-13, 64, 90
breaching 60
breathing 21, 49
breeding 48-53
breeding groups 35
Britain 91, 92, 93
British Columbia 60-1
'bubble nets' 71
bubble-rings 28

California Bight 58
calves 35, 48-53, *48-9*, *51*, 59, 73
Cambodia *13*
Canada 60-1, 91
Cardigan Bay 89
cetaceans 9, 15
Chile 59
chimpanzees 28, 80, 83
China 13
clicks
    communication 40, 43
    echolocation 22-5, *24*, 27

colour 11
colour vision 25
Commerson's dolphin 12, 58
common dolphin 11, *20*
    feeding 58, 60, 61, *66-7*, 71
    lone dolphins 52
    mixing with other species 40
    navigation 24
    schools 88, *88-9*
    shark attacks 73
    social groups 33
    teeth 61
communication
    calves 51
    emotions 44
    gestures 79-83
    language 29, 41, 76, 77, 79-82
    posture 44, 47, *47*
    research 77, *78-9*, *79*, 85-6
    signature whistles 40-1, *41*
    sounds 40-3, *41-3*, 79-83
    touch 44-6, *46*
Communication Research
    Institute, St Thomas 76
cornea, eyes 25
Cortez, Sea of *71*, *88-9*
courtship 43
Cousteau, Jacques 73
'crater dives' 60

Dall's porpoise *14*, 92
death 52-3, 90-2
Delphinidae 11
Dingle Bay 52
diseases 92
DNA 15, 84
Dolphin Research Center,
    Grassy Keys 80
Dolphin Research Institute,
    Melbourne 87
dolphinaria 77
dominance *27*, 35-8
dorsal fins 9, 15, 49
drag 17, 21
drift nets 90
dusky dolphin 6, 12, *20*
    deaths *93*
    feeding 60, 61, 62-4
    home range 39

hunting 56
    lone dolphins 52
    social groups 38

ears 23, 25
Earthtrust *77*, *77*
Earthwatch *29*, *81*, 89
echolocation 21, 22-5, *22-4*
    brain and 27
    evolution of 15
    and feeding 57, 58, *59*, 60,
        62, 64, 69, *70*
    and fishing nets 90
    research 77
emotions 27-8, 44
encephalization quotient (EQ) 28
English Channel 88-9
evolution 15
eyes 25, 64, 90

false killer whale 9-11, 12, 33
family life 31-53
fat reserves 92
feeding 49-50, 51, 54, 55-70, *59-71*
females
    breeding 48-53
    hierarchy and dominance 35
fighting 38, *38*
finless porpoise 14
fins 9, 15, 49
fish, hunting 25, 51, 54, 56-70,
    59-71
'fish thwacking' 65
fishing boats 70, 71, 86-7, *90-1*
fishing nets 90-1, *90-1*
flippers 25, 46, 65-9
Florida 39-40, 48, 52, 58, 69,
    83-6, 89
food chain 92
Fort Meyers Beach 86
fovea, eyes 25
franciscana 12-13
Fraser's dolphin 12
Fungie 52, *52*

Galveston Ship Channel 69-70
gangs 44
genitals 25, 46-7, 48
gestation 48

gestures, communication 79-83
'ghost nets' 90, *90-1*
Gibraltar, Straits of 88
Great Barrier Reef 69
grey whale 40

habitats 11-13
harbour porpoise *14*, 52
Hawaii 21, 71, 73, 77, *78-9*, *79-80*
'head turn' 47
hearing 25, 69
heart rate 21
Heaviside's dolphin 12, 82
Hector's dolphin 12, *90-1*
herding behaviour, hunting 60-1,
    62-4
Herman, Louis *82*
hierarchy 35-8
high-energy sounds 58
home ranges 39-40
hourglass dolphin 11, *11*
Human–Dolphin
    Communications Project 78-9
Humane Society *93*
humpback dolphin 12
    mixing with other species 40
    research 86-7
    and sharks 73
    social groups 33, 38
hunting 25, 32, 54, 56-70, *59-71*
hydrophones 82, 85, 86

ichthyosaurs 15
Iki Island 92
Indian Ocean 12
infanticide 52-3
intelligence 26-9
Ireland 52
Irrawaddy dolphin *13*
isoveric acid 22

Japan 38, 58, 92
jaws 9, 14, 22-3, 57, *57*

Kaikouru 6, *93*
Kealakekua Bay 32
Kewalo Basin Marine Mammal
    Laboratory 79-80, *81-3*
killer whale (orca) 9-11, 32

feeding 60-1, 57, 70
    as predators 64
    and sharks 73
    social groups 33, 38

La Plata River 12-13
lactation 49-50, 59, 70, 92
laminar flow 17
language 29, 41, 76, 77, 79-82
lantern fish 57, 59
lenses, eyes 25
life span 53
Lilly, John 76
lone dolphins 52
long-finned pilot whale 40, 57
Long Marine Laboratory,
    California 86
Los Angeles 58
Loyer, Bertrand 8
lungs 21
Lydonia canyon 58

magnetite 24
males, hierarchy and dominance
    35-8
Malta 73
mammary slits 48
Marineland, San Diego 77
Marten, Dr Ken 77
mating 46, 48, 53
Mediterranean 73
Mekong River *13*
melon (forehead) 9, 21, 22, 64
melon-headed whale 12, 33
memory 29, 82-3
Mexico, Gulf of 39-40, 92
Miami Seaquarium 73
microvibrations 17-20
milk, suckling 49-50, *49*
mimicry 29, 40-1, 76, 83
Miocene period 15
mirrors, self-awareness tests
    28-9, *78*
Misha 87
Monkey Mia 88
monkeys 28
Moreton Bay 71, *72*, 86-7
Mote Marine Laboratory 86
muscles 17

names 40-1
narwhal 14, 15
navigation 24
nerves 17, 23
nets, fishing 73, 90-1, *90-1*
New Quay Dolphin Monitoring
  Group 89
New Zealand 6, 12, 38, 52, 93
nipples 50
noise pollution 93
North Atlantic Ocean 11, 12, 58
northern right whale dolphin
  11-12

Old Charley 88
Old Speckled Belly 88
Opo 52
orca *see* killer whale
Orinoco River 12
ovulation 48
oxygen, breathing 21

P&O European Ferries 88-9
Pacific Ocean 12, 59, 71, 73, 90-1,
  93
Peale's dolphin 12, 59
pectoral flippers 25, 46, 65-9
penguins 57
people and dolphins 75-93
pheromones 26
pilot whale 9-11
  calves 51
  distribution 12
  feeding 57, 70
  life span 53
  and sharks 73
  social groups 33
plankton 20-1, 58, 92
Platanistidae 11
play 28, *28*, 43
poisons 91-2
pollution 91-3
porpoises 13-14, *14*, 52, 92
porpoising *16-19*, 21, *21*
Port Philip Bay 87
posture, communication 44, 47, *47*
predators 52, 64, 71-2
pregnancy 48, 92
Project Delphis *78-9*

Project Pod 86
purse seine nets 90-1, *91*
pygmy killer whale 12, 89
pygmy sperm whale 15

Queensland 71, 86-7

radio transmitters 84
'red tide' plankton 20-1, 70
ribcage 21
right whale 40
right whale dolphin 9, 11-12
Risso's dolphin 12, 38, 52, 57
river dolphins 11, 14, 64
  distribution 12-13
  evolution 15
  feeding 64
roll calls 32, *62*
'rostrum rides' 46-7
rough-toothed dolphin 12

Sagan, Carl 76
San Diego 58
Sarasota Bay 39, 48, 51, 52, 71, 89
Sarasota Dolphin Research
  Program 84-6, *85*
satellite tracking 84
scars 38, *38*, 71, 72-3
schools, hunting 60
Scotland 38, 52, 64
Sea Life Park, Hawaii *77, 77*
sea lions 61
Sea World, Orlando 74
seals 57, 61, 92
self-awareness 28-9, 78
senses
  echolocation 22-5, *22-4*, 27
  eyesight 25, 64
  hearing 69
  smell 26
  taste 26
  touch 25, *26*, 44-6, *46*
sex 46, 48
Shark Bay 44, 65, 72-3
sharks 8
  attacking dolphins 32, 40, 52,
    71-3
  evolution 15
  feeding 70

shrimps 58, 70, 86
signature whistles 40-1, *41*
size 9-11
skin 17-20
  scars 38, *38*, 71, 72-3
smell, sense of 26
social groups 33
social intelligence 27-8
sonar *see* echolocation
sounds
  communication 40-6, *41-3*,
    79-83
  echolocation 22-5, *22-4*, 57
  high-energy 58
  noise pollution 93
  research 85-6
South Africa 38, 73, 82
South America 12-13, 39
Southern Ocean 11
southern right whale dolphin 12
species 11-13
speed 16-17
sperm whale 15, 40
spinner dolphin *10*, 11
  distribution 12
  feeding 59, 60, 61, *61*
  mixing with other species 40
  roll calls 32, *62*
  shark attacks 71
sponges 28, 65
spotted dolphin *10*, 11, 34-7
  breeding 48, 50, *50*
  communication *41-3*, 43,
    44-6, *45, 47*
  distribution 12
  dominance hierarchy 27
  feeding 58, 59, 60, *60*, 61, *70*
  lone dolphins 52
  research 83
  sense of touch *26*
  and sharks 73
  social groups *30*, 40, *40*
  speed 16
  suckling *48-9*
squid 48, 57, 58
striped dolphin 11, 89
  diseases 92
  feeding 58
  social groups 38

suckling 49-50
swimming 16-21, *16-19*

tails
  'fish thwacking' 65
  tail slaps 47
Tampa Bay 86
tapetum lucidum 25
taste, sense of 26
teeth 9, 14, 51, 57, *57*, 61
television, research 78, 80, 83
temperature, body 17
Texas 57-8, 70
threat displays 47
toothed whales 13, 15, 91
touch
  communication 44-6, *46*
  sense of 25, *26*
toxins 91-2
toys 28, *28*
travel 39-40
trawlers 70, 71, 86-7, 90-1
tucuxi 12, 52, 64
tuna 54, 59, 90-1
turbulence 16-17, 20-1

ultrasound, and feeding 62
Uruguay 12-13
US Naval Oceans Systems
  Center 21
US Navy 93

Virginia 52, 53
vision 25, 64

watching dolphins 87-9
Whale and Dolphin
  Conservation Society 93
whales 9, 13, 14, 15, 21, 89
whistles, communication 40-1,
  41, 43, 51
white-beaked dolphin 11, 38, 61,
  64
white-sided dolphin 12, 40
white whale 14, 15
Wild Dolphin Project 83, 84, 89

Yangtze River 13, *15*